Teaching Writing in Middle School

Teaching Writing in Middle School

Tips, Tricks, and Techniques

Beth Means

Lindy Lindner

Teacher Ideas Press
An Imprint of Greenwood Publishing Group
361 Hanover Street
Portsmouth, New Hampshire
1998

TEACHER IDEAS PRESS
An Imprint of Greenwood Publishing Group
361 Hanover Street
Portsmouth, NH 03801
1-800-225-5800

Production Editor: Kevin W. Perizzolo
Copy Editor: Jason Cook
Proofreader: Susie Sigman
Typesetter: Kay Minnis

Library of Congress Cataloging-in-Publication Data

Means, Beth, 1949-
    Teaching writing in middle school : tips, tricks, and techniques /
Beth Means, Lindy Lindner.
    xiv, 209 p. 22x28 cm.
    Includes bibliographical references (p. 199) and index.
    ISBN 1-56308-562-3
    1. English language--Composition and exercises--Study and teaching
(Middle school)--United States. 2. Creative writing (Middle
school)--United States. I. Lindner, Lindy, 1945- . II. Title.
LB1631.M399   1998
808'.04'0712--DC21   97-39412
                                                                CIP

To

CASEY and RON

for paying the phone bills

With special thanks to Marcia Olsen, Anne Helmholz, Bob Carey, Dr. Nancy Pokorny, and Martha Means for patient reading and testing; to Alice Greiner and Maureen Aumen for "The Paragraph Puzzle"; to Carolyn Lacey Turner, our long-suffering bird dog on sources and errors; to our students whose work appears as samples in the book; especially to our teachers, Henriette Anne Klauser for freeing the artist within and Betty Hagman for training the craftsman; and finally, to all the writers from Virgil to Gary Paulsen who wittingly or unwittingly came along for the ride.

Contents

6 ∽ **EDITING WITH ENTHUSIASM** (*continued*)

Introduction

HOW TO TEACH WITH THIS BOOK

Even practical, day-to-day writing is both an art and a craft. It's an art because its driving force is the inspiration of the writer. It's a craft because it demands skill, patience, and practice to do well. This book is designed to help you and your students explore the basic aspects of writing. We divide the long, complex writing process into more manageable pieces: planning, drafting, and editing. We further divide planning into two parts: deciding what to write about (Chapter 1) and more-detailed planning (Chapter 2). We also use a three-step editing process (Chapter 6): revision, polishing, and presentation. The book is organized according to the writing process, so that you can easily find activities on whatever piece of the writing process you would like to explore with your students.

We wrote this book by collecting ideas from adults who write professionally and then adapting them for use as activities in the middle school classroom. Of course, a great idea on paper does not necessarily turn out so well in a real classroom, so we field-tested the activities. Beth uses them in her writing workshops with sixth-, seventh-, and eighth-grade students, and Lindy and her fellow teachers have been using them at Mrachek Middle School in Aurora, Colorado, for the past six years. From these experiences we feel confident that these strategies, lessons, and activities are easy for teachers to use and engaging for students. Each activity has a brief introduction, with an appropriate epigraph, and a bit of history or some idea you might want to present to students. This is followed by the instructions we give to students and the handouts we use.

At the end of each chapter, except for chapters four and five, we have included a section called the "Teacher's Notebook," which has ideas on teaching writing generally or on teaching the activities in that chapter. The professional writers we interviewed or studied gave us all sorts of ideas about writing that can help teachers and students. We have included some of the best in the "Notes from the Pros" section at the end of each chapter, following the "Teacher's Notebook."

Three of the "Teacher's Notebooks" are of special interest when you are organizing your class. We have our students keep two notebooks and a folder: one notebook is for collecting writing ideas and a second larger notebook for writing practice paragraphs and rough drafts. The folder for final copies we call the portfolio. All of our students have a writing group that they work with on drafting and editing. We start younger students in pairs until they have some practice working with others in the groups. In any case, the groups are limited to four students. In student instructions we may say "get out your practice notebook" or "work with your writing group." You can substitute your particular organizational methods for ours. If you want more details on ours, see "Teacher's Notebook: On Keeping a Writing Ideas Notebook" and "On Personal, Practice, and Portfolio Assignments" in chapter one and "Teacher's Notebook: On Writing Groups and Writing Conferences" in Chapter 2.

COPING WITH THE TIME PROBLEM

You will never have enough time for writing. No one ever does, but you can use the writing process itself to help you get the most out of the writing time you have. We don't take every piece of student writing all the way through the writing process. We suggest that you guide students all the way through the process using some very short pieces first. Once they understand the stages of the process, you can isolate particular aspects of it for more practice or in-depth attention. For example, first sentences require lots of practice—much more than students will ever get from writing one good first sentence for a few complete pieces. We turn the process around. First, we use "Hooks and Leaders" (Chapter 3, Activity 6) to help students write as many as twenty first sentences. Then we might choose one of those sentences to begin the drafting of a full-length piece. If we want to emphasize research and planning, we might spend a lot of time on the research, then recycle it by using one piece of research as the basis for a variety of writing pieces. Because recopying or retyping and then "publishing" takes as much time as the rest of the writing process put together, we limit the number of pieces each year that go all the way through the final polishing "publication." (See "Teacher's Notebook: On Personal, Practice, and Portfolio Assignments," Chapter 1.) If you have enough computers, word processing can sometimes save time on the final printing. You might also time-share with other teachers; for example, a social studies teacher might guide students through the research and planning, and then a language arts teacher might direct the drafting and editing. Be ever vigilant for ways to save time for writing—you will need them.

FICTION OR NONFICTION?

Both! Students learn more vocabulary, problem solving, and punctuation with fiction. They learn about audience, structure, clarity, and paragraphing with nonfiction. Be sure to use the full range of nonfiction as well. Academic nonfiction teaches students the dispassionate voice, clarity, and factual accuracy. No middle school teachers worth their salt wants to send students off to high school who do not know how to write a decent school paper. However, writing movie reviews or articles for a school magazine is often more useful than expository or academic nonfiction, and beginning writers will learn just as much about structuring nonfiction and *more* about audience from nonacademic nonfiction. Sometimes, so little time is set aside for writing that students only do school papers. This is a big problem because, in our experience, students' ability to learn certain kinds of writing varies with age. Seventh-graders are natural novelists. Once they have written something—anything—that they can call a chapter, they are unstoppable. Sixth-graders prefer short stories and how-to pieces. Eighth-graders are best at nonfiction magazine-style articles and opinion pieces, such as book, movie, and music reviews. You should take advantage of their natural inclinations. When students are enthusiastic about the subject, they are more interested in learning technique. In general, if we are trying to teach them something about writing, we let them choose the subjects. If the purpose of the paper is to help them increase their knowledge of a subject by writing about it, we try to let them choose the type of writing. The most important goal is an overall balance, so that they have ample opportunities to practice, to try several different genres, to write fiction and nonfiction, and to take a few trips through the entire writing process, including "publishing" some of their best work.

GETTING STARTED

If you have not used this book before, try a few activities from Chapter 3 first. "Brain-dancing and Downhilling" (Activity 3) and "Zoom Lens" (Activity 5) are good places to begin; then use "Follow the Leader" to show students models of good writing. Use "Zoom Lens" again to help them focus on the details they will need to write their pieces. This will give you a taste of the activities in the book and show you how you can combine them or use them alone. You can pick activities, like recipes, to work into the writing you are already doing, or you can pick one or two activities from each chapter and construct a complete trip through the writing process around them. (Remember to use very short pieces to start.) Chapter 4, "Nonfiction Workshop," shows you how you can combine activities from throughout the book to teach nonfiction writing. Alternatively, you could use the activity "Weaving Scenes" and the elements of fiction in Chapter 5 to create an in-class fiction workshop.

We do have favorite activities that seem to work well, either in small writing workshops, or classes of forty squirming bodies trapped two to a desk, with sixth-graders to college students. They are our classics. You may find your own favorites as you become familiar with the book, but this selection should get you started.

Chapter 1: Deciding What to Write About

The most important concept in this chapter is the Writing Idea Triangle (covered in more detail at the beginning of Chapter 2). It helps you design your assignments, and it helps students begin to understand the large number of choices they make—consciously or unconsciously—each time they write. Our favorite activity is "Stop, Look, and Listen" (Activity 1). If we only have a few students in a writing workshop, we send them around the school. For a big group, we put posters on the wall to enrich the environment. You might also borrow two minutes from the beginning of any field trip to have students make a "stop, look, and listen" list. On a slow day, or one of those days when the students are bouncing off the walls, we make "Stop, Look, and Listen" lists, then do five-minute fastwrites until the bell finally rings.

Chapter 2: Planning

We recommend "Prewriting Choices for Nonfiction" (Activity 1), "Prewriting Choices for Fiction" (Activity 2), and "Research Strategy" (Activity 4) for the seventh and eighth grades; and "The Knowledge Chart" (Activity 3) and "Making a Pictionary" (Activity 7) for the sixth grade. Most of the activities in this chapter are also good study and research techniques.

Chapter 3: Getting the Words to Flow on Paper

We usually combine either "Creative Concentration" (Activity 2) or "Zoom Lens" (Activity 5) with "Follow the Leader" (Activity 8) for starters. You can use this combination with any other activities to introduce students to writing concepts, to give them practice, and to build their confidence. You can find samples for "Follow the Leader" in books the students are reading or in almost any piece of good writing. Don't worry about finding examples that are at your students' writing level. Choose things well above their reading level—you'll be surprised at what they can do.

Chapter 4: Nonfiction Workshop

In middle school, students receive their first taste of nonfiction writing, and an introduction to academic nonfiction or expository writing. Teaching this is not an easy task because students this age haven't yet fully developed an ability to connect cause and effect, and they don't yet have many facts to command. They also haven't read much nonfiction, so they don't have an intuitive sense of nonfiction the way they do with stories. In this chapter, we present two activities, "Topics and Sluglines" (Activity 1) and "The Paragraph Puzzle" (Activity 2), that can be used again and again with many nonfiction assignments to help with these difficulties. Add a little patience, and you'll see improvements in students' nonfiction writing.

Chapter 5: Fiction Workshop

When we are trying to push students to write longer pieces, we like to begin with fiction. Use the activity in this chapter to help students "weave scenes" using action and dialogue. Add description and introspection. Then try all four. Once students are familiar with weaving together the basic elements, introduce some of the more detailed ideas, such as foreshadowing and flashback. When they have several scenes to connect, they can tackle transition writing.

Chapter 6: Editing with Enthusiasm

The most important thing that students should learn from this chapter is that editing has three distinct parts: revision, polishing, and presentation. Presentation is one of the most time-consuming parts of the process, so we tend to revise and polish the pieces, then put them in a folder. Later, we'll select pieces from the folder to type and illustrate for the portfolio or "publication." Papers written for other classes provide opportunities for revision, polishing, and presentation. The key activity in Chapter 6 is "The Revision Loop" (Activity 3). "Teacher's Notebook: On Grading Papers" is worth special consideration: It presents a grading system that allows you to push students to do their very best work, but in a positive, helpful way that doesn't produce unnecessary writing anxiety.

Teaching writing to a classroom of bouncing thirteen-year-olds or bored fourteen-year-olds is not easy, but what they learn in middle school and high school about the art and craft of writing will affect their opportunities for schooling, jobs, and self-expression for the rest of their lives. We salute every teacher who undertakes the task, and we hope that every one of you finds something in this book that helps.

Deciding What to Write About

> Waiting for inspiration is like waiting for friends. If you sit around the house and don't go out and meet them, they will never come. You have to make things happen. Writing is an active occupation, not a passive one.
>
> —Judy Delton

INTRODUCTION

Like many adults, children often think that their lives are too dull to write about, that writers must be special people—minor gods who drop books into the library by magic. "Did your hair freeze off when you were in the Arctic?" one of our students seriously asked an author, apparently surprised that a writer, like a parent or a teacher, could be bald.

Ask published writers where their ideas came from and, time and again, they will point to some small incident in everyday life that they enlarged, or something they read in a newspaper or book. Marcel Proust conceived the ideas for the Swann stories while placing a teacup in its saucer. Agatha Christie claimed that her best ideas came while doing the dishes. They discovered writing when they discovered that they did not need to lead a special kind of life to write.

Students need to know that the stories and books they see in the library are the creations of ordinary people like themselves. Even the simplest life is rich with starting points for writing. The details that make fiction sing and nonfiction concrete come from the commonplace world that surrounds each of us. Because no two people lead the same life or see life the same way, each person's writing is indeed special. The writing club is open to everyone. To join, all one needs are a few ideas.

The Writing Idea Triangle

The first task of the writer is to decide what to write about, that is, to develop a specific writing idea. The Writing Triangle helps students understand the elements that come together to make a good writing idea (see fig. 1.1).

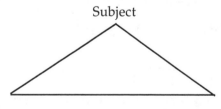

Subject

Type or plan
(e.g., fiction, nonfiction or
a genre, an outline, etc.)

Other elements of the writing
(e.g., mood, purpose, setting,
characters, audience, etc.)

The Writing Idea Triangle.

Any point of the triangle can serve as a starting point, but two points, and usually all three, are needed to make a writing idea. For example, any subject can serve as a starting point for an infinite number of writing ideas. The subject may be horses, but the writing idea needs something more:

a character:	Horse named Looney Tune
a setting:	Horse ranch
an explanation:	How to groom a horse
an opinion:	Why I don't like horses
a question:	What was the economic importance of horses in the nineteenth century?
a design:	Descriptions of horse breeds arranged alphabetically by name

The writing idea may come from the type of writing. When we asked a group of students who were studying the ancient Egyptians to develop writing ideas about the pyramids, they suggested the following:

story:	A day in the life of an Egyptian pyramid builder
how-to:	How to build a pyramid
explanation:	Why the Egyptians built pyramids
tips:	Five problems with building a pyramid in your backyard

Even a narrowly defined topic can be a starting point for writing ideas. For example: Why did Hannibal fail as a military leader?

Hannibal failed because he ran out of money.

Hannibal failed because he was too far from home.

Hannibal failed because his men didn't like him.

Who can forget Will Cuppy's wonderful idea:[1]

Hannibal failed because he refused to admit that elephants always run backwards in the face of enemy fire.

We explain to students that they need to develop a writing idea before they write anything (except for a personal journal entry) because a story or a nonfiction piece is more than a collection of paragraphs—it is a collection of paragraphs unified by one idea. This central idea distinguishes a scrawl from a story, and one story from another.

---

1. *The Decline and Fall of Practically Everybody* (Lincoln, MA: Godine, 1984).

Our rule is that a teacher or a publisher may assign the starting point, but developing the writing idea is always the responsibility of the writer. This rule helps students narrow their topics, and it gives them a stake in their writing. Enthusiasm is an indispensable tool of the writer; a sense of choice and a sense of responsibility are essential to enthusiasm. We have another, equally important rule we tell our students: Don't sit around waiting for ideas to come to you. Go out and find them!

The activities in this chapter are divided into two parts. The activities in part 1 are designed to help students find starting points for writing—principally subjects—in the world around them. The activities in part 2 are designed to help students develop starting points into writing ideas by adding other writing elements or by choosing a type of writing.

PART 1:
FINDING YOUR OWN STARTING POINT

Even a small room containing only a table and a bed is full of writing subjects: the bedframe, mattress, table legs, table drawer, wall, floors, and windows. It would be possible to write an entire, interesting book on the history of mattresses from the cave man to the present or a short story about the person living in that room. The activities in part 1 are designed to help students notice those subjects around them and to write them down. They can later choose subjects from theirs lists to develop into writing ideas.

Activity 1:
Stop, Look, and Listen

> There is only one trait that marks the writer. He is always watching. It's a kind of trick of mind he is born with.
>
> —Morley Callaghan

The beauty of "Stop, Look, and Listen" is its simplicity. Anyone can do it in a minute or two. Students can use it at school, at home, on field trips, or on vacation.

Instructions to Students

In your "Starting Points and Writing Ideas Notebook," write down ten things you see and ten things you hear. Don't be picky—anything will do—and work quickly. It won't take you more than a minute or two.

After you have finished the list, pick a few items. Do they suggest any writing ideas or questions that might become writing ideas? Note the writing ideas at the bottom of the page; mark them clearly, so you can find them later.

EXAMPLE

Starting Point

(A list made while sitting in a classroom after school.)

See		**Hear**	
1.	desk	1.	lawn mower
2.	tennis shoes	2.	freeway noise
3.	picture of an Amazonian frog	3.	ruffling pages
4.	grass	4.	siren
5.	pencil	5.	computer printer
6.	sink	6.	"Who put the coffee grounds in the sink?"
7.	computer	7.	"This school is a mess."
8.	glasses	8.	giggling girls
9.	hand	9.	whack, whack of library cart

Writing Ideas

Desk: Why do they make those little half-desks instead of full-size desks? Is it to cram more kids into a classroom like passengers on a no-frills airline? Who thought up the idea? The answers to these questions might make an interesting research piece or a good, funny piece speculating on crazy reasons or uses for half-desks.

"This school is a mess": Interview the school janitors about their problems with keeping the school clean, and write a list of ways students and teachers could help janitors. Write a science paper about the chemicals used in cleaning products.

Glasses: Visit a local optometrist to learn how glasses are made, how optometrists are trained, or why people decide to become optometrists. Write a funny poem explaining why glasses get sat on. Write a paper for health class explaining how glasses help people see.

Additional Notes to Teachers

There are many ways to use "Stop, Look, and Listen" lists. Try some of these variations on the theme:

- Make the lists in specific places, such as a museum, an airport, a train, a plane, a classroom decorated to reflect a subject, a field trip location, or a favorite place.

- Make the lists at specific times, such as during a film or television show, during a classroom activity or laboratory, during a school assembly, before sleeping or after waking, during vacation, or every day at (for example) 4:35 p.m.

- Make the lists in response to an interesting piece of art, music, dance, or photography.

- Add "ten things you think" to the list of things seen and heard.

- If cameras and cassette recorders are available, take pictures and make audio recordings of the items in the lists. Use the pictures and cassettes to inspire writing or to present or illustrate the final written products.

- Limit the list to specific types of starting points. Art teachers might limit the list to things of a certain size or color. Science teachers might limit the list to things that express certain principles of physics, chemistry, or math. Music teachers might limit the list to things heard—soft sounds, rhythmic sounds, or sounds expressing a particular mood.

Activity 2:
This Is Your Life

〜Writing comes more easily if you have something to say.

—Sholem Asch

There is an old rule among writers: "When you are learning to write, first write about yourself, the things you know, and your own experiences." It is still a good rule. We use starting points from "This Is Your Life" for assignments focused on practicing technique rather than content.

Students enjoy this activity and often want to keep writing. Although the purpose of this activity is to collect writing ideas, allow enough time for students to write while the inspiration is hot. They can return to collecting starting points and writing ideas after the desire to write cools.

Instructions to Students

Write your answers to the questions from the "This Is Your Life" handout (p. 8). This is not a test. We ask your opinions about many things. Answer honestly. We also ask you to remember events in your life. If you can't remember, close your eyes and think for a minute, then write down the first answer that comes to you. If you still can't remember anything, make up an imaginary answer. When you have finished, review your answers and find at least three starting points. Note any writing ideas as well. Select any answer and write about it for a few minutes.

This Is Your Life

<u>Student Handout</u>

1. What event or experience in your life would you like to write about?

2. What is your favorite food?

3. What food do you hate the most?

4. Name three things you like to do. Why do you like doing them?

5. Name three things you hate doing. Why do you hate doing them?

6. Name two places you especially like to be. Why do you like being there?

7. Name two places you dislike being. Why do you dislike being there?

8. If you could do anything you wanted, what would you do?

9. Name two things you have never done but would like to try.

10. What is the best thing you have ever done?

11. What is the worst thing you have ever done?

12. What is the funniest thing you have ever done?

13. Do you own a pet? If so, list some of the things your pet does.

14. List the names of your brothers and sisters. List some of the best, worst, and funniest things they have ever done.

15. Name two things that scare you.

16. Name two things that make you happy.

17. List three changes you would make if you were in charge of the world.

18. What is your earliest memory?

19. List any five things you know.

20. List any five things you don't know.

21. What is your favorite book? What is the best part?

22. Answer question 1 again.

23. (Write a question to yourself about your life and answer it.)

Activity 3:
Borrowing Lists

ᔪ Research is to see what everybody else has seen,
and to think what nobody else has thought.

—Albert Szen-Gyorgyi

This activity is an excellent way to introduce students to the reference section of the library—a good thing in itself as well as a good source of starting points.

Instructions to Students

Choose a book from the library. Let any book fall open to a page and write down five words, facts, or opinions from that page. Or, let the book fall open to five different pages and write something from each page. Some books are especially interesting: Try using a dictionary, encyclopedia, book of lists, or book of quotations. If you can't find them, ask the school library media specialist for help.

Dictionaries: Any word in a dictionary can be a starting point. Special dictionaries are particularly intriguing: *Morris Dictionary of Word and Phrase Origins* (three volumes) by William Morris and Mary Morris is full of fascinating information. For example, the word *motel* was invented by an architect in San Luis Obispo, California, in 1925. Although *kid* means "a young goat," it has been used as an affectionate name for children since Shakespeare's time. According to H. L. Mencken's *The American Language*, another useful reference, *kid* is used in American English for "co-pilot."

Try subject dictionaries. Science, art, music, law, computers, writing, and publishing dictionaries can be found in most libraries. *The People's Chronology: A Year-by-Year Record of Human Events from Prehistory to the Present*, edited by James Trager, is wonderful for finding historical starting points. Try *What's What: A Visual Glossary of the Physical World* by Reginald Bregonier and David Fisher, a dictionary with pictures and correct names for things such as venetian blinds.

Encyclopedias: Try short encyclopedias, such as *The New American Desk Encyclopedia* (1984) from Signet's New American Library, or books of lists, such as Irving Wallace's *The Book of Lists #2*, Isaac Asimov's *The Book of Facts*, and *The Teacher's Book of Lists* by Sheila Madsen and Bette Gould.

Books of Quotations: Quotations provide good starting points for writing. Most people think of Bartlett's *Familiar Quotations*, but Bartlett's is arranged by author. Quotation books arranged by subject are often more interesting. Good examples are *Dictionary of Quotations* by Bergen Evans, *The International Thesaurus of Quotations* by Rhoda Thomas Tripp, and *Peter's Quotations: Ideas for Our Time* by Laurence J. Peter. Books of quotations on particular subjects are also available.

PART 2:
DEVELOPING STARTING POINTS
INTO WRITING IDEAS

The trick to developing a good writing idea is to develop several ideas and then choose the best. The activities in Part 2 help students develop many writing ideas from any one starting point. The activities should be played like games. The object is to think of several writing ideas, no matter how dull or silly they may seem. One can usually find a good writing idea in any list of four or five ideas. Most of the activities can be done individually, in small groups, or as a class.

Activity 4:
The Three-Minute Fastwrite

> ∽ Just as appetite comes by eating, so work brings inspiration, if inspiration is not discernible at the beginning.
>
> —Igor Stravinsky

Three minutes of concentrated writing is a substantial amount of time to a writer. A person's first thoughts about a starting point are often the most original and powerful. Simply writing down first thoughts for three minutes is one of the easiest ways to generate the best writing ideas. The first time you introduce fastwriting, choose the simplest of starting points: We suggest "breakfast," "the best time of the day," and "school."

Instructions to Students

In your practice journal or on a sheet of paper, write as fast as you can for three minutes about a starting point. When you fastwrite, always use a pen that flows freely and feels comfortable in your hand.

Don't try to write well. Write the first things that come to mind. Don't cross out anything. If you change your mind, make the change in the margin or at the bottom of the page. We will be using "The Three-Minute Fastwrite" often during the year; this first time is practice. We'll assign a starting point, start a three-minute timer, and say "Go." After three minutes, we'll assign another starting point. Ready? The first starting point is "breakfast." Go.

Review your fastwrite and note any writing ideas you have at the bottom of the page.

Additional Notes to Teachers

The three-minute fastwrite has many classroom uses (time can be found to do a fastwrite every few days even during the busiest of weeks). A fastwrite can be used as

- a daily fluency exercise,
- a way to help students begin a new assignment,

- a way to consolidate students' understanding of a lesson,

- a "sponge" activity to introduce or conclude a lesson and help students absorb more of the lesson,

- a pause during a social studies or science class to help students understand the subject.

Activity 5:
Fiction, Nonfiction, or Poetry?

> ～ Nonfiction is saying, "I caught a 12-inch fish." Fiction is saying, "I caught the biggest trout I ever saw before." In a lot of ways, fiction is more true than nonfiction.
>
> —Gary Paulsen

Unlike botanists, writers have never organized their terminology into consistent classes, families, and species. But three principle types of writing can be defined simply: fiction, nonfiction, and poetry:

Fiction: Fiction is a written work based on the writer's imagination. Fiction includes short stories, novels, plays, radio and television scripts, and other writing, except poetry, in which the people, places, and events of the story are created from the writer's imagination. The imaginary people in fiction are called characters, the imaginary places are called settings, and the imaginary events of a story are called the plot.

Nonfiction: Nonfiction is a written work based on either fact or opinion. Nonfiction is the largest category of writing. Nonfiction includes essays, opinion pieces, magazine and newspaper articles of all kinds, letters, diaries, histories, biographies, and even cookbooks and dictionaries. Almost everything that is neither fiction nor poetry is nonfiction.

Poetry: Poetry is the most personal of all writing. Poet A. E. Housman said, "I could no more define poetry than a terrier can define a rat." Still, a terrier knows a rat when it sees one, and most people recognize a poem when they see one. A piece is a poem because the writer says it is a poem. Poetry is not necessarily writing that rhymes, although some poems do use rhyme. Poetry also includes writing to be sung— ballads, hymns, musical comedy, and opera.

Instructions to Students

Choose any starting point and write down a fiction idea, a nonfiction idea, and a poetry idea. Writing ideas often come to mind in the form of fiction or nonfiction. Choosing one of the three categories is an easy way to develop a starting point into a writing idea.

EXAMPLE

Starting Point

(A paragraph about a blind dog named Alice, from a "This Is Your Life" activity.)

Alice is blind. She carries her bowl around in her mouth when she wants food. She comes to work with me. Sometimes she waits in the shower or stands on my shoes in the morning when she wants me to hurry. She also snores. She can find her way out of any yard or building. The worst thing she ever did was dump a gallon bottle of cooking oil on the living room rug.

Writing Ideas

Fiction: "My Dog Wears Purple Tennis Shoes," a story about Alice getting ready for work

Nonfiction: How to care for a blind dog

Poetry: A poem based on my feelings when Alice went blind

Activity 6:
The Genre Game

> ～ An idea is a feat of association.
>
> —Robert Frost

"The Genre Game" is popular with students. The word *genre* comes from the French language, meaning "type." It refers to similar pieces of writing. It is most often used for types of fiction, but it applies to nonfiction as well.

There are hundreds of genres in fiction and nonfiction. New genres and subgenres develop continually. Explain to students that genres are not precise types. Genres develop because writers like a particular author's work and then use similar ideas in their work. For example, the mystery genre was inspired by Wilkie Collins's novel *The Moonstone*, stories by Edgar Allen Poe, and Sir Arthur Conan Doyle's Sherlock Holmes stories. So many writers have used this genre since then that subgenres (e.g., the detective mystery, the English mystery, the adventure-mystery, etc.) have developed. For nonfiction, the essay genre was invented by Michel de Montaigne, a seventeenth-century lawyer and crank who retired to a real ivy covered tower to write his *Essaies*.[2] The French verb *essayer* means "to try." Montaigne's notion was to use each essay to try to examine one idea or theme. Since then, the formal essay, the informal essay, the personal essay, the general academic essay, and specialized academic essays have developed as subgenres.

Instructions to Students

Review the handout "Starter List of Genres." Write down one writing idea for each genre. Don't worry about how good the ideas are, just try to think of something. If you don't know much about the genre, it helps to write down what you do know before playing the game. After you have finished, check off the ideas you like most.

---

2. Currently available from Penguin Classics.

Starter List of Genres

<u>Student Handout</u>

Popular Fiction Genres

Adventure: Stories in which characters must overcome danger

Choose Your Own Ending: Stories in which the reader is the main character in the story and can choose their actions

Fantasy: Stories set in imaginary kingdoms, or stories about mythical beasts or characters with special powers

Historical Fiction: Stories set in the real historical past but with imaginary characters or plots

Horror: Scary stories

Mystery: Stories about solving a mystery

Nostalgia: Stories based on memories of a character's past

Romance: Stories about falling into or out of love

Science Fiction: Stories set on imaginary planets, in imaginary societies, or in the future

Tall Tale: Exaggerated accounts of a real or imagined event

Popular Nonfiction Genres

Autobiography: The life story of the writer

Biography: Life stories of interesting people

Collection: Collections of a specific type of information (e.g., a dictionary is a collection of word definitions and spellings; a cookbook is a collection of recipes)

Consumer: Tips on buying, selling, or repairing

Essay: Pieces presenting, explaining, or arguing for one idea or theme (subgenres are informal, which is often humorous; formal; personal; and academic)

History: Pieces that explain the history of people, places, things, or ideas

How-To: Explanations of how to make or do something

Information: Straightforward presentations of facts

Nostalgia: Pieces based on memories of the writer

Opinion: Pieces in which the writer expresses an opinion and makes a case for it

Personal Experience: Pieces based on an event or problem in the lives of real people

Profile: Pieces about an interesting person or group of people

Reporting: Newspaper-style explanations of current events

Self-Help: Pieces discussing how to help yourself overcome personal problems, such as getting bad grades or not having friends (self-help pieces are similar to how-to pieces, but with less emphasis on step-by-step instruction).

Note to poetry fans: this activity, in the authors' opinion, does not lend itself to poetry, even though there are many genres of poetry. That is why it is not included in the genre game.

From *Teaching Writing in Middle School*. © 1998 Beth Means and Lindy Lindner. Teacher Ideas Press. (800) 237-6124.

To play the genre game, write the names of the fiction and nonfiction genres down the left-hand side of the page, followed by a list of the things that inspire poetry. Write your writing ideas down the right-hand side of the page. (Note to teachers: the younger the students, the shorter the list of genres they should use to play the game. Start with five or six with sixth graders, especially the first time they play.)

EXAMPLE

Starting Point

Amazonian frog (from a "Stop, Look, and Listen" list)

Writing Ideas

Fiction Genres

Adventure: A story of a fishing trip to Brazil that goes awry when one of the party tries to catch a frog

Choose Your Own Ending: Your spaceship has crashed on the Frog Planet (oops)— What do you do next?

Fantasy: A story about a little boy whose pet frog can tell him the future

Historical Fiction: A story set in Brazil at the turn of the century

Horror: A story where weird, scary things happen every time the frogs start croaking

Mystery: A story in which an Amazonian frog skin is used as a murder weapon

Nostalgia: "Summer of the Amazon," a story of a boy's summer in the Amazon River Basin

Romance: A story of a frog biologist who falls in love with a reporter who is writing an article about his work

Science Fiction: A story of life on a jungle planet

Tall Tale: "The Great Frog Leg Rebellion," a story of a dinner during which the guests are served frog legs, to their distress

Nonfiction Genres

Autobiography: An autobiography that explains why I have never been interested in frogs

Biography: A biography of the first anthropologist to work among the Amazonian Indians

Collection: A collection of class frog stories and articles

Consumer: Ten tips to help consumers avoid buying endangered species of frogs that have been imported illegally

Essay: A comparison of Amazonian frogs to North American frogs

History: A history of the discovery of a rare species of frog in the Amazon

How-To: How to study frog anatomy

Information: How the Indians of the Amazon live

Nostalgia: Memories of my father reading stories about the Amazon and my dreams of going there

Opinion: Why we should protect rare species

Personal Experience: "Frogs in the Basement," a true tale

Profile: "The Man Who Loves Frogs," a story of a biologist who studies Amazonian frogs

Reporting: A report of the biology class project about Amazonian frogs

Self-Help: "Overcome Your Fear of Frogs"

Activity 7: Who, What, Why, When, Where, and How

∽ I keep six honest serving men
(They taught me all I knew);
Their names are What and Why and When
And How and Where and Who.

—Rudyard Kipling

Following a simple, structured procedure can bring ideas to mind by giving one's imagination a little push. This exercise is especially useful for nonfiction ideas. We often use it on Friday afternoons when the class is too tired to feel imaginative.

Instructions to Students

In your "Starting Points and Writing Ideas Notebook," write down your starting point at the top of the page. Write down a question about your starting point beginning with *who, what, why, when, where,* or *how.* Reread the question and write down two related questions or comments.

Return to your starting point and repeat the process. If you used *what* to write your first question, use *who, why, when, where,* or *how* for your next question. Work away until you have at least one question beginning with *who,* one beginning with *what,* and so forth. Note any writing ideas at the bottom of the page. Silly questions are allowed—even encouraged.

EXAMPLE

Starting Point

freeway noise (from a "Stop, Look, and Listen" list)

Questions

Where does the noise come from? The wheels or the car engines? Bumps on the surface of the road?

What have people been doing to reduce noise from freeways? Building fences? Planting trees? Tearing up old roads?

How does noise affect people? Does it make them sick? Can too much noise ruin your hearing? How much is too much?

When is it noisiest? At night? Rush hour? Last day of school?

Who studies noise? Engineers? Doctors? Who else?

Why does noise exist? What makes sound? What stops sound? Is there any sound in space?

Writing Ideas

A factual nonfiction article or story about whether or not there is sound in space

An article on the effect of noise on people and animals

EXAMPLE

Starting Point

pencil (from a "Stop, Look, and Listen" list)

Questions

How do they get the lead into the middle of the pencil? It's such a tight fit, you would think it grew that way. Do they have special machines to drill the holes?

When you plant a used pencil in the ground, will a new pencil grow? Do the pencil makers plant pencil seeds to grow new pencils?

Where are the pencil forests? Do they use leftover trees or big, newly cut trees to make pencils? Maybe they glue scraps of wood together.

What kind of trees make the best pencils? Fir trees? Pine trees? Hardwoods?

Why do pencils always break or disappear just before you begin a test or write a phone message? Does somebody train them to disappear, or is it "pencil instinct"? You never throw away pencils, but they never seem to be around when you need them. Where do they go?

Who invented the pencil? What was the inspiration? Did the same person invent the pen, too?

Writing Ideas

The history of the lowly pencil

A humorous essay titled "The Truth About Pencils"

An information piece explaining how pencils are made

Activity 8:
People, Places, and Problems

> 〜Whatever pulls you to it like a secret magnet may be your story meat. Your imagination is a mysterious and somewhat holy place.
>
> —Paul Darcy Boles

This activity is the fiction equivalent of "Who, What, Why, When, Where, and How." It is based on arbitrarily inventing a character, a setting, and a problem for the character to solve.

Instructions to Students

Divide a sheet of paper into four columns, using the headings "Starting Point," "Person" (character), "Place" (setting), and "Problem" (central conflict). To play this game, think of a starting point, a person, a place, and a problem for the person to solve. Use the starting point to suggest the person, place, and problem, or create these details independent of the starting point. Give the person a name, if you haven't done so. Write, "This is a story about a _____ , named _____ , who _____" and fill in the blanks.

EXAMPLES

(From a "Stop, Look, and Listen" list.)

Starting Point

desk

Person	Place	Problem
boy	sitting at desk	lost homework

This is a story about a boy named Jim, who is always losing his assignments and has just discovered that he has lost his social studies homework for the third time in a row.

Starting Point

siren

Person	Place	Problem
elderly lady	house near hospital	hates sirens

This is a story about an elderly lady named Florence, who lived in London during the Blitz and can't stand sirens.

Starting Point

ruffling pages

Person	Place	Problem
librarian	sailboat	bored

This is a story about a librarian named Jack, who is bored with his job and wants adventure. One day on his way to work, he is attracted by an advertisement seeking a cook for a sailboat going on a race around the world.

Starting Point

This school is a mess.

Person	Place	Problem
girl	Xenon, a messy planet	a tidy person

This is a story about a student named Jeso, who goes away to school on the planet Xenon and is disgusted that the school—and everything else—is a mess because Xenonites don't care about litter. So she goes on a crusade to change their ways.

Activity 9:
Wacko

∽What happens to the hole when the cheese is gone?

—Bertolt Brecht

"Wacko" is so named because the wackier your mood, the more fun you have. We play "Wacko" with students even when they aren't developing writing ideas. This is a fun group game that calls for a certain amount of inspired lunacy.

Instructions to Students

From your "Starting Points and Writing Ideas Notebook," choose a fact, an opinion, or an observation from any of your lists. Make it "go wacko" by turning the idea upside down or changing it around. Let your first wacky idea inspire other ideas, and keep going until you run dry. One of your wacky ideas might develop into a good writing idea.

EXAMPLE

Starting Point

I hate zucchini. (from a response to a "This Is Your Life" question list)

Wacky Ideas

Suppose I liked zucchini. Suppose zucchini liked me! Could zucchinis be trying to get my attention? Is that why they grow to forty pounds overnight if I fail to pick them each evening? Is that why zucchinis appear on my doorstep or my desk when I'm not looking?

Writing Idea

"The Zucchini Conspiracy," a silly story about what zucchinis really do when people aren't looking

EXAMPLE

Starting Point

"From all levels of government, federal, state, and local, Americans get 150,000 new laws and two million new regulations every year." (from Isaac Asimov's *Book of Facts*)

Wacky Ideas

Suppose a country could only pass one law each year. What law would people choose? Most people would probably choose "love thy neighbor" as the best law. Would it work? Maybe not.

Writing Idea

A fictional newspaper article from *The National Snoop*:

> (*Anywhere, U.S.A.*) Mr. Jake Blunt, owner of the Flat Earth Deli and Gas station, was hauled into Superior Court today and charged with two counts of Not Loving Thy Neighbor. Blunt allegedly snarled at his neighbor on two separate occasions for not returning Blunt's borrowed lawnmower. Blunt was found guilty on both counts and paid a $100.00 fine.
>
> "There oughta be a law," growled Blunt at reporters afterwards. Reporters reminded him there was a law: "Love Thy Neighbor."
>
> "Yeah?" replied Blunt. "Well it's not all it's cracked up to be."

Additional Notes to Teachers

◆ Remind students that sometimes ideas come to mind in entire paragraphs and stories. Write it while the inspiration is hot! (It oughta be a law.)

TEACHER'S NOTEBOOK

On Keeping a
Writing Ideas Notebook

Nothing is more reassuring than a pocketful of starting points and writing ideas. We ask our students to keep a "Starting Points and Writing Ideas Notebook" for writing assignments and personal journal entries. The starting points and writing ideas resulting from the activities in this chapter are written in the notebook. A 3-by-5-inch spiral-bound notebook is ideal because students can carry it wherever they go. Some students might enjoy using word-processing or database software to create an online notebook, to exploit the cross-referencing power of the computer.

On Personal, Practice, and
Portfolio Assignments

One way to increase the amount of practice students receive without increasing the paper storm that always accompanies writing assignments is to have students keep all rough drafts in either a personal journal or a practice journal, and all polished pieces in a portfolio. Students share their personal journal drafts only when they wish; practice journals are turned in for teacher review by a few students each week; polished pieces go in a student's portfolio. Portfolio pieces are fully polished and presentable pieces ready for "publishing," which we define as any way the piece is presented in public. This system calms the paper storm and reduces number of papers the teacher must read, and it encourages students to keep their writing, even their unedited writing, over a long period of time. P. G. Wodehouse observed that success in writing comes so gradually that writers are always surprised at their progress when they look back. If students toss out their assignments, they will never have the chance to see their progress.

There are always a few students in every group who discover the joy of writing through the personal journal. Some students have trouble writing because they worry too much about the teacher's expectations and, as a result, write correct but dull pieces. Others are convinced that they lack imagination and need the luxury of a personal journal before they will attempt fiction or poetry. Those with poor self-esteem often gain enthusiasm and confidence that might otherwise escape them. Knowing that they need not show their perceived "failures" to anyone helps them separate writing from editing—or the expectation of editing. This improves their fluency and makes writing less painful.

The practice journal is the most important—and overlooked—learning tool for the novice writer. Curiously, people expect young violinists to squeak away in practice and young golfers to muff shot after shot at the driving range, but they forget that young writers also need the same kind of small-scale, private practice and plenty of stray practice shots. Young musicians are also taught to isolate small sections of a work and practice the section again and again, whereas young writers are rarely told about the importance of repeated practice of writing and rewriting an isolated paragraph of dialogue, a description, or a conclusion. By keeping all their rough drafts and their practice paragraphs in a journal, students learn to practice writing properly, to expect a certain amount of failure, to keep practicing, and to edit their work before they share it outside their writing group. A quick scan through a practice journal gives the teacher a much better sense of a student's progress, attitude, and problems than reading one paper in a pile.

Every novice writer must learn to revise and polish a draft into a quality piece of which they are truly proud. In our experience, students get more out of polishing one C piece into an A piece than by turning in five unpolished C pieces, so we limit the number of portfolio assignments and set fairly high standards for a piece before it can be put into the portfolio. To encourage students to edit, we give them the chance to edit and revise any piece until it meets portfolio standards, after which we hold a brief class celebration to honor a student's effort. Writing is hard work; students deserve applause for success. This system reduces the time students waste typing, and allows more time for practice or revision.

We recommend using a grading system based on personal, practice, and portfolio assignments (see "Teacher's Notebook: On Grading Papers," Chapter 6).

NOTES
FROM THE PROS

On Falling in Love and Burning Out

Writing begins with passion—passion for the subject, passion for the genre, passion for the ideas. Passion is the engine that drives writing. Without it, writers cannot sustain the energy to finish. Writers who work contractually in the same genres, writing about the same subjects again and again, often burn out. Sir Author Conan Doyle killed Sherlock Holmes to escape from the genre and the character. Other writers have stopped writing altogether. Wise writers, if they feel themselves burning out, begin anew, with a genre and a theme of their choosing, with passion.

Students do not truly learn to write until they fall in love with a story, a genre, a subject, or an idea and write about it with all their heart. It's a great moment. Unfortunately, most students never experience this moment because school curriculums often teach the process backwards. Students are assigned "papers" on specified topics again, and again, and again. They burn out before they ever fall in love.

If you want your students to enjoy writing, remember that passion comes first. Let them choose what to write about and how to write it again and again. Do not reserve creative writing for the "best" students. Creative writing is writing; students need to discover passion before they will improve. Move forward with writing activities, so that students can try new genres, new subjects, and new ideas. Teach them terms and techniques one day; let them write without direction the next. Have them write practice pieces; have them write complete pieces. Above all, avoid the burnout assignment. Then wait patiently for them to fall in love.

Planning

INTRODUCTION

When most people think of writing plans, they think of an outline. English teachers faithfully teach the outline and usually ask students to turn it in with the finished piece. If asked, students will admit that they often write their outlines after finishing the drafts. There is nothing wrong with this. Outlines are excellent revision tools. The problem with outlines is that they don't necessarily help the novice get started writing.

Beginning a piece of writing feels like pinning clouds to a bulletin board. It's hard to know what to tack down first. Every student asks the same questions: How can I research before I know what I am going to write? How do I know what to write until I outline? How can I outline until I know what I am going to write?

It's difficult to advise students how to proceed. Nowhere are experienced writers less consistent than in preparing to write. They talk about it; they refuse to talk about it. They make outlines; they hate them. They write 70,000-word summaries; they try to find just one word. They barely research; they collect volumes of information. They begin drafting from the beginning and write to the end; they won't begin drafting until they finish the last page. They plan little by little between drafting sessions; they plan everything before they begin. They call what they do before they write by a thousand different names: planning, outlining, research, narrowing the topic, finding a slant, preliminary drafts, prewriting, and incubating. Every writer and every piece is different—not a reassuring or helpful thought for a beginner wondering what to do next with a handful of clouds.

Teachers often try to help students with story-starters or narrowly defined topics. Usually, though, this doesn't work. Only a few students in any group are inspired by the story-starter or the topic, and none of them learn to think for themselves. In the long run, it is better (and easier) to cover each point of the Writing Idea Triangle (see Chapter 1, p. 3) at least once. After all, what all writers really want from planning is a crystal-clear writing idea. Once you gently lead students all the way through the planning process, you can joyfully toss the story-starters and narrowly defined topics out the window.

The Writing Idea Triangle
Revisited

Each piece of writing is a new adventure. No one can anticipate everything with planning. Students, who have not had much writing experience, are even less likely to know what to plan for. The three points of the Writing Idea Triangle give them an easy way to organize their planning into steps. Covering all three points, at least briefly, ensures that students cover the ground that they might come upon once they begin writing. (For introductory purposes we simplified in Chapter 1 the names of the points of the triangle. They really are focus, background, and order.)

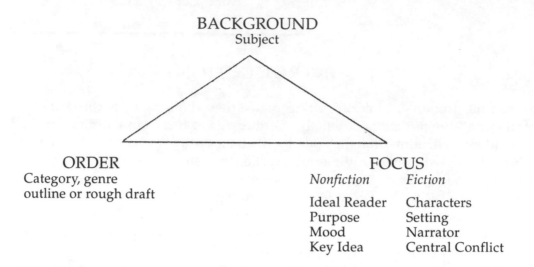

The Writing Idea Triangle Revisited.

Choosing important elements of the writing helps students find a focus for their piece. Researching the subject gives students the background material and vocabulary needed to write fluently. Because writing is sequential, the "order" point of the triangle includes anything that gives the writer clues about what will come first and what will come next. It can be as vague as a genre or as specific as a first rough draft. Outlines fall somewhere between.

In theory, thoroughly tacking down each point of the Writing Idea Triangle would clarify the idea to the point where drafting the piece would be secondary, and no revision would be necessary. In practice, the plan may never be finished until the third or fourth revision.

The background of a piece is large and vague. Without guidelines, students flop around in pools of information, never quite knowing what to do with it all. The prewriting choices, however, are specific. They are easy to make. Choosing them early narrows the field of research considerably, so we usually begin at the "focus" point of the triangle, then move to researching for the background. We always tackle the "order" point of the triangle last—if at all. It is the most difficult point for students and writers alike. Many people must begin by writing and then organize while they edit. In theory, one could begin at any point of the triangle; in practice, focus, background, then order usually works best.

The activities in this chapter are divided into three parts: "Finding a Focus," "Background Research," and "Finding an Order." Each contains a potpourri of useful prewriting activities and handouts. We consider Activities 1 and 2 absolutely necessary because they introduce students to the prewriting choices.

We have found that leading students through the planning process the first time is much easier if you begin with very short pieces about ideas of their choosing. Make sure nonfiction students choose a simple subject with which they are familiar. If possible, steer them toward genres with a strong sense of order, such as how-to, tips, question-and-answer, and so on. Avoid biographies, reports, essays, and other complex genres. Steer fiction students toward stories with one or two main characters in a familiar setting.

PART 1:
FINDING A FOCUS

The prewriting choices have two things in common: They are crucial decisions all writers must make, and accidentally changing even one of them in the middle of the draft will always result in a major rewrite or a confusing disaster. Writing involves many decisions, but these particular choices operate a little like the artist's horizon line and perspective points. They aren't terribly difficult choices to make, but choosing them aligns the perspective for the rest of the work. They make writing so much easier for students that we consider them the most important contribution we make to a student's writing. The prewriting choices are:

Nonfiction	Fiction
Ideal Reader	Characters
Purpose	Setting
Mood	Narrator
Key Idea	Central Conflict

Activity 1:
Prewriting Choices for Nonfiction

> ∼i can never think and write at the same time/
> nobody can do two things at the same time/
> and do them both well
>
> —Don Marquis

There is an old saying among writers: "Nonfiction starts hard and ends easy; fiction starts easy and ends hard." It's true for students, too. They have a terrible time beginning nonfiction and an equally hard time finishing fiction. Teachers first give students long nonfiction assignments in middle school, and it's a hard start. More often than not, the results look like scrambled eggs with minced encyclopedia.

Stories can grow from what happens first and what happens next. That rarely happens in nonfiction. Developing a clear focus is ninety percent of the nonfiction battle. Once students get off to a little easier start, many of them prefer writing nonfiction, and their work always improves. In this activity, we present a nonfiction prewriting choices worksheet and an instructional handout to help students.

These handouts are long. If your budget is short for such things, you can use the prewriting worksheet and give a verbal explanation. We like to send the handouts home with students because few stories are finished without a little help from Mom and Dad. Parents are often grateful for clues on how to help their children without writing the piece for them.

Instructions to Students

When you write, you make many decisions. You make little decisions, such as what word to use in a sentence, and big decisions, such as choosing a writing idea. There are certain other decisions you should make before you begin writing. For this reason, we call these decisions the prewriting choices. For nonfiction, you choose your ideal reader, purpose, mood, and key idea. You don't know it now, but you'll see later that making these decisions early makes writing nonfiction much easier.

Sit with your writing group today. On the "Nonfiction Prewriting Choices" handout is an explanation of each choice. As you make decisions for your piece, record them on the worksheet and discuss them with your writing group. Write in pencil, so that you can change your decisions if necessary.

(Text continues on p. 33.)

Nonfiction Prewriting Choices Worksheet

<u>Student Handout</u>

My writing idea is: _____

_____

_____ .

Ideal Reader

My ideal reader is: _____ .

I chose this ideal reader because: _____

_____

_____ .

Purpose

The purpose of this piece is to: _____

_____

_____ .

My ideal reader would like to read this piece because: _____

_____

_____ .

Mood

The mood of this piece is: _____ .

Key Idea

My key idea is: _____

_____

_____ .

Nonfiction Prewriting Choices

<u>Student Handout</u>

Ideal Reader

Who is going to read your piece? Thinking of one particular person as you write helps you decide what to write. Suppose your writing idea is "how to make a peanut butter and jelly sandwich." You would write one thing to a five-year-old, who has never made one, and something completely different to a cafeteria worker, who has made hundreds.

When you choose an ideal reader, you can choose a real person or make up an imaginary person. It is usually easier to choose someone who knows less about your subject than you; for example, someone younger than you, someone who is learning about your subject for the first time, or one of your fellow students who hasn't read about it yet. Don't choose your teacher. You will keep wondering what to write that the teacher doesn't already know. When you choose your ideal reader, ask yourself, Why do I know more about this than my ideal reader? It helps.

Purpose

Why are you writing this piece? Why would your ideal reader want to read it? Do you want to entertain your reader? To show your reader how to do something? To persuade your reader to do something? To describe something your reader hasn't seen? Answer these questions, and you will know your purpose.

Think of your writing as a gift. You give your gift to your ideal reader. Your purpose is what you plan to give.

Examples

To *entertain* my ideal reader

To *show* my ideal reader *how something works*

To *show* my ideal reader *how to do something*

To *persuade* my ideal reader *to do something*

To *report* to my ideal reader *something that happened*

To *give my opinion about something* to my ideal reader

To *explain* to my ideal reader *why I have a particular opinion*

To *describe something* to my ideal reader

To *trace the history of something* for my ideal reader

To *show* my ideal reader *why (or how) two things are the same*

To *show* my ideal reader *why (or how) two things are different*

You can have two purposes; for example, "to explain how to do something in an entertaining way," "to give my opinion and explain why," or "to describe something and trace its history."

Mood

A piece of writing is like a good conversation. It shares a mood as well as ideas. You can be friendly and helpful. You can go on a crusade for your ideas. You can be detached and logical. You can be funny and informal. Think of sitting down with your ideal reader over lunch and talking with him or her about your writing idea. What kind of mood do you want your conversation to have?

EXAMPLES

angry	friendly	leisurely
commanding	helpful	quick
critical	humorous	sad
crusading	informative	serious
detached	ironic	silly

Key Idea

Your key idea is your writing idea. Any article, essay, or book should be about just one key idea. Everything else in the piece is somehow related to that idea. To choose your key idea, you can use your original writing idea as is or sharpen it using the decisions you've made about the ideal reader, purpose, and mood. The sharper your idea, the easier it is to write nonfiction.

EXAMPLES

Original Writing Idea

How to make a peanut butter and jelly sandwich

Key Ideas

How to make forty peanut butter and jelly sandwiches in no time flat

How to make your first peanut butter and jelly sandwich

How to make low-calorie peanut butter and jelly sandwiches

A day in the life of a peanut butter and jelly sandwich

Original Writing Idea

What freedom means to me

Key Ideas

Gives people rights and responsibilities

Must be practiced everyday

The little things in life

Having dreams of your own

A story of one person's escape to freedom

Original Writing Idea

Getting good grades

Key Ideas

Why students should try to get good grades

A survey asking teachers why they give grades

Ten tips for getting better grades

What to do when you get a bad grade

A story of a person's first A

Sharpening your key idea takes a little practice. Sometimes it helps to pretend that you are holding a camera. Suppose your subject is trees. Are you going to write about the big, wide-angle picture and trace the history of an entire forest? Or are you going to use a narrow lens and focus on the history of just one tree in that forest? Perhaps you'll write the history of something in the middleground—one type of tree in that forest or all the trees along one stream.

Think, too, about the period of time you will write about. If you will be writing about one tree, are you going to cover its entire history, back to the Ice Age? Or are you going to show what happens to and around that tree during spring, summer, fall, and winter? What about just one day in the life of that tree?

It sometimes helps to think of several key ideas that might work, then choose the best one. Remember to choose just one key idea. You should only write about one idea at a time. Two key ideas will make your piece confusing and hard to write.

Activity 2:
Prewriting Choices for Fiction

⌁Why shouldn't truth be stranger than fiction?
Fiction, after all, has to make sense.

—Mark Twain

To anyone who loves writing, teaching twelve- to fifteen-year-olds to write fiction is a great joy. They never run out of ideas, their enthusiasm is infectious, and their capacity for absorbing some of the technical aspects of writing fiction is astonishing. Seventh- and eighth-graders may be a little shaky on nonfiction, but fiction is ice cream and candy to most of them.

Better yet, writing fiction pressures them to develop their vocabularies and encourages them to use more complex sentences. The logical demands of fiction stress connecting cause and effect. Students may learn more about science from writing science fiction and more about history from writing historical fiction than they will from writing reports or essays. Fiction is an ideal vehicle for teaching middle school and early high school skills and concepts. Teachers don't use it enough, or use it creatively enough.

Students this age have no trouble creating plots. They'll stuff every story with four or five plots. "But I may never get to write another story," one student complained when we pointed out that he had enough characters and plots for ten stories. It's really impossible to plan stories too far ahead, so the principle purpose for the fiction prewriting choices is to help students sort out just one story to write.

These handouts are long. If your budget is short, you can use the prewriting worksheet with a verbal explanation of the choices. We like to send the handouts home with students along with a note to parents to save them. Few writing assignments are complete without a little help from parents and the handouts give them clues on how to help without doing the writing.

Instructions to Students

Sit with your writing group. Today we're going to learn to make the prewriting choices for fiction: characters, central conflict, setting, and narrator. On the "Fiction Prewriting Choices" handout is an explanation of each choice. As you make decisions for your piece, record them on the worksheet and discuss them with your writing group. Write in pencil, so that you can change your decisions if necessary.

(Text continues on p. 38.)

Fiction Prewriting Choices Worksheet

<u>Student Handout</u>

My writing idea is: _____

_____.

Characters

The full name of my main character is: _____.
My main character wants: _____.
The names of my secondary characters are:

_____.

_____.

_____.

Central Conflict

The central conflict of my story is: _____

_____.

The story ends when: _____

_____.

The crisis comes when: _____

_____.

The story begins when: _____

_____.

Setting(s)

My story is set in (the big setting or settings): _____

_____.

List possible little settings within the big setting(s):

_____.

_____.

_____.

_____.

The main setting is _____important/ _____secondary.

Narrator

My narrator (first person) is the character in my story named: _____.
My narrator (third person) is a person outside my story who is retelling it, named:

_____ .

Story Statement

This is a story about: _____

_____

_____.

Fiction Prewriting Choices

<u>Student Handout</u>

Characters

Stories are about imaginary people. Even if your story is about animals or creatures from another planet, the animals or creatures act like people. The imaginary people, animals, or creatures in your story are called characters. The most important characters in your story are your main character and your secondary characters.

The Main Character

The most important character in your story is called the main character. You can only have one main character. The main character has a problem to solve, wants something, or tries to do something. This is called the central conflict. In *The Wizard of Oz*, for example, Dorothy wants to get home to Kansas. In *E.T.*, E.T. wants to phone home. In the Sherlock Holmes stories, Holmes wants to solve the mystery. Your first prewriting decision is to choose your main character. What does your main character want? That's your central conflict.

The Secondary Characters

The secondary characters are the other important characters besides the main character. For example, the Tinman, the Scarecrow, and the Lion are secondary characters in *The Wizard of Oz*. Elliot, the little boy who helps E.T., and Dr. Watson are also secondary characters. You can choose just one or two secondary characters or a whole crowd of them.

The difference between the secondary characters and the main character is that the central conflict belongs to the main character. The Tinman and Scarecrow help Dorothy get back to Kansas. They just happen to solve some of their own problems along the way.

You don't need to have a secondary character, but be careful not to have too many. One or two is usually more than enough to make a good story.

Minor Characters and Bit Players

There are two other types of characters that you should know about, although you don't need to make any decisions about them now. You can make them up as you write. These are minor characters and bit players.

Minor characters usually have names. The reader learns a little bit about them, but not much. For example, the Wizard and all the witches in *The Wizard of Oz* are minor characters. Villains are often minor characters. In *E.T.*, Elliot's mother is a minor character. Sherlock's clients are minor characters.

Bit players, though, are hardly people at all. They do their little bit for the story and disappear. They open the gates to Oz, drive taxis to the airports, answer questions at hotel desks. They usually don't even have names.

If you think of your main and secondary characters as being "round" (that is, the reader knows all about them in detail), your minor characters and bit characters are "flat." Your reader never learns very much about them; they are just there to move the story forward in some way.

From *Teaching Writing in Middle School.* © 1998 Beth Means and Lindy Lindner. Teacher Ideas Press. (800) 237-6124.

Central Conflict

The central conflict is your main character's biggest problem. It's easiest to think of a central conflict by asking yourself, What does my main character want? Does he or she want to do something? To solve a problem? To get something? To make something? The answer is your central conflict. When your main character gets what he or she wants, your story ends. (Sometimes your main character doesn't get what he or she wants. In this case, the story ends once it's clear that the main character will never get it.)

Beginners often make the mistake of creating several central conflicts. Stick to just one. Just because you choose one central conflict doesn't mean there won't be plenty of other problems for your characters to solve. Dorothy didn't make it home to Kansas without bumping up against witches and dark forests. Secondary characters have their problems, too. The Tinman wanted a heart, and the Scarecrow wanted a brain. The central conflict, the problem that started all these problems, was Dorothy's desire to go home.

Think of your story as a series of stair steps building up to a high point. Each step forward is another step to solving the main problem, but each step also has complications or setbacks to overcome. The story builds up to a final, big setback—a crisis. All seems lost. Then the main character overcomes the last setback, the central conflict is resolved, and the story quickly ends.

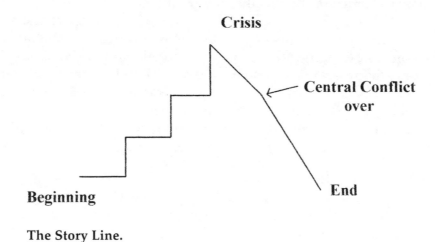

The Story Line.

Because you know that the story ends once the central conflict is resolved, it may help you to first decide how the story will end. Then decide what the crisis will be and, last of all, how to begin.

Setting(s)

Your characters are who your story is about. The central conflict is what your story is about. The setting is where your story takes place.

Your story may have one setting or several settings. If you have more than one, it helps to think of settings as big settings and little settings. The big setting might be a town. The little settings might be the school, the local hardware store, or the town square. Your big setting might be a country. The little settings might be a city in that country, a small town in the mountains, or a roadside café on a main highway. If you are writing a science fiction story, your big setting might be another planet. The little settings might be various places on that planet.

You can have more than one big setting, but try not to use more than two or three. Once you choose a big setting, think of two or three smaller settings within the big setting.

How important is the setting to your story? If your story is set in an unfamiliar place, such as another planet or a far off country, your setting might be very important. If your setting is uninteresting, such as a house that could be anywhere, the setting may not be important at all. You decide.

Narrator

You have one more imaginary person to create before beginning your story—the narrator. The narrator is the person who tells the story. Of course, in real life, you tell the story because you made it up, but readers like to pretend that stories really happened. They want to know how the person telling the story knows it. Is the narrator a character in the story who knows about it because he or she was there? Or is the narrator someone who found out about it who is retelling it.

If you pretend to be a character telling the story, your narrator will use *I* to tell the story. This is called a first-person narrator. If you pretend to be someone who found out about the story but wasn't part of it, your narrator will tell the story using *he* or *she*, not *I*. This is called a third-person narrator. (The third-person narrator is sometimes called the omniscient narrator. *Omniscient* means "all-knowing." The omniscient narrator knows what every character did and thought.) The next time you read a story, notice the narrator. Is it a first-person narrator or a third-person narrator? (Do not worry about the second person narrator. Few stories are written in second person.)

EXAMPLES

> I walked the dog and then went to the store. (first-person narrator—a character in the story named Mary)

> Mary walked the dog, and then went to the store. (third-person narrator)

Here are two good rules to follow:

1. Create whatever narrator you like, but stick with the same narrator all the way through the story.

2. Pretend that your narrator is telling the story after the story has ended (past tense). Don't pretend that your narrator is telling the story as it happens (present tense). It's hard to tell stories in present tense.

EXAMPLE

> I *walked* the dog, and then *went* to the store. (past tense)

> I *walk* the dog, and then *go* to the store. (present tense)

PART 2:
BACKGROUND RESEARCH

Young students are long on imagination but short on information and vocabulary. With students between twelve and fifteen, the process of research is almost as important as the product. It's more than collecting information. Young students feel a great deal more pressure when they write than do adults because the physical process of writing is so much more painful for them. Research gives them a chance to talk through possible sentences without having to write them down, a sort of rough draft without the draft. Talking about the background helps them develop the vocabulary they will need to write the story.

All background research should include reading and as much talking about it as possible. In general, the more students talk when they plan (and the less they talk when they draft), the easier writing is. (See also "Notes from the Pros: On Talking About It," Chapter 3.)

The first two activities in this part help students decide what to research. The third helps them find readily available "experts" to interview. The fourth helps fiction students round out their major characters. The last three help students develop their vocabulary.

Activity 3:
The Knowledge Chart

> ∾ As is our confidence, so is our capacity.
> —William Hazlitt

Breaking the subject into bite-sized chunks is always the best first step to research. We use this simple activity to help students chart what they know and what they don't know about a subject or a writing idea, so they can think about what information they need to gather.

Instructions to Students

Now that you've made your prewriting choices, you have a focus and you know what you are going to write about, but what are you going write? Well, you might have some ideas, but you don't have all of them yet. Today, we're going to begin researching the background for your stories and nonfiction pieces. Think of your key idea or your central conflict as the foreground. To fill in all the details, you need to study the background. Nonfiction writers research the subject; fiction writers research the setting or the details of the characters' lives. Research not only helps you think of things to write, it also gives you confidence. You know what you are writing about because you read about it and thought about it before you began writing.

Where do you begin your research? Make a list of the things you already know about the subject. What about the things you don't know? Make another list. Finally, make a list of things you need to learn. It's that simple. To make it even easier, use the "Knowledge Chart" to help you record your lists in one place.

Those of you writing nonfiction should make lists about your subject: peanut butter sandwiches, hot air balloons, turtles, and so forth. Fiction writers should make lists about the setting, the history of the characters, or some event in the story.

EXAMPLE

NAME: JB Student
WRITING IDEA: Raising Turtles as a Hobby
DATE:

WHAT I KNOW	WHAT I DON'T KNOW	NEED TO FIND OUT

- Reptiles
- Like water, mud
- Have hard shells
- Several types
   snapper
   box
   green
   tortoise
- they are an old species
	- how they fit in the ecological chain
	- what they eat
	- how old they get
	- which types make good pets
		- ecological chain
		- foods for different types of turtles
		- oldest turtle
		- why make good pets and why not
		- what makes a good pet
		- where to buy the best types

The Knowledge Chart.

Activity 4:
Research Strategy

〜 Time given to thought is the greatest time-saver of all.

—Norman Cousins

Research is an art of its own. Without help, few students get much beyond copying the encyclopedia at this age, yet to write, they need the information research yields. What teachers need is a simple way to get students started. We use a research strategy. Like the "Knowledge Chart" example (see Activity 3 above), it breaks the research into manageable tasks, but it also introduces students to the idea of using different sources and encourages them to interview people, make their own observations, and use books other than the encyclopedia.

Instructions to Students

Research is a fancy sounding word for collecting facts, ideas, and information. You can research by reading books, talking to people, or observing something yourself. These books, people, and observations are called sources.

You could just go to a library and read any book about your subject, but even the school media center is a big place. You can't read every book. You need to choose a few. Just talking to anybody won't do. You need to find an expert who knows what you want to know. What you need is a strategy to help you decide what to read and who to consult.

There are three parts to a research strategy: areas, pointers, and sources. Areas are broad categories you want to study. Pointers are ideas of what to study within each category. Sources are the books you read or the people you ask.

EXAMPLE

NAME: JB Student
WRITING IDEA: What to do when you get a bad grade
DATE:

AREAS	POINTERS	POSSIBLE SOURCES
What to do	What do teachers say student should do?	teachers
	What do good students do?	good students
	What do poor students do?	poor students
Bad grade	What is a bad grade?	Counselors
	Why do teachers give bad grades?	teachers
		Survey of student opinion

Research Strategy.

(Text continues on p. 44.)

How to Create a Research Strategy

Student Handout

There are four steps to creating your research strategy:

Step 1: Break your story statement or key idea into areas to study.

Step 2: Make a list of pointers.

Step 3: Make a list of possible sources.

Step 4: Make a notebook and choose priorities.

Step 1: Break your story statement or key idea into areas to study.

From your "Prewriting Choices Worksheet," copy your story statement or your key idea statement on a separate sheet of paper. Underline all the important words and phrases in your story statement or key idea. Make a list using these words. If you are not sure whether or not a word is important, underline it. You can always cross it out later.

EXAMPLE

Nonfiction

Key Idea

<u>What to do</u> when you get a <u>bad grade</u>

    what to do
    bad grade

Fiction

Story Statement

This is a story about some people who <u>crash</u> their <u>plane</u> in the <u>Amazon</u> and <u>fight</u> their way through the <u>jungle</u> back to a <u>small town</u>.

crash	fight
plane	jungle
Amazon	small town

Now you have a list of the areas you want to study.

Step 2: Make a list of pointers.
(Note: If this is too difficult, use a "Knowledge Chart" first.)

Bad grades, crashes, and planes are big subjects. You won't need to know everything about them for your story. Pointers narrow the subject areas and point out the types of things within that area you might want to learn. Write a few pointers for each area.

From *Teaching Writing in Middle School*. © 1998 Beth Means and Lindy Lindner. Teacher Ideas Press. (800) 237-6124.

EXAMPLE

Nonfiction

Areas	Pointers
what to do	What do teachers say students should do?
	What do good students do?
	What do poor students do?
bad grade	What is a bad grade?
	Why do teachers give bad grades?

Fiction

Areas	Pointers
crash	What makes planes crash?
	What would the pilot do in a crash?
plane	What kind of plane would be a good one for the story?
	How many passengers do various small planes hold?
Amazon	What part of the Amazon has jungle near it and a small town?
	What sort of people live in the Amazon? What language do they speak?
	What's the weather like?
fight	What sort of tools and supplies would be needed to survive, say, ten days in the jungle?
	What kind of food would the passengers be able to hunt or find? How would they go about it?
jungle	What does it look like?
	What are the names of some of the plants?
	What are the dangers of the jungle?
small town	What does it look like?
	Would it have an airport? Boats?
	Would the town people be different from the jungle people?

Step 3: Make a list of possible sources.

There are three types of sources:

Experts: An expert doesn't need a Ph.D. An expert is just a person who might be able to answer questions you have about the area you are researching. For example, you could talk to a pilot about planes and airplane crashes. You might know someone who visited the Amazon on vacation.

Personal Observation: You can make yourself into an expert by taking a look yourself and making notes. If you will be writing about peanut butter and jelly sandwiches, try making one for research. You could go to the Amazon, if you could afford the trip, but you could also watch a television program about the Amazon and take notes. You can also look at planes in a local museum or your local airport. Observation also includes doing experiments and taking surveys.

Books, Articles, and Films: Almost everything you need can be found in some library somewhere. The school media center is a small library. Your local public library is bigger. There are also some huge libraries, such as the Library of Congress. Show your research strategy to the media center specialist, who can help you choose the proper books, articles, and films to find the information you need.

Look at each area on the list and think about the kinds of questions you need to answer. Is there an expert nearby you could interview? Can you personally observe something or take your own survey? Are there books, articles, or films you could read or see? Next to each area, write down the possible sources.

EXAMPLE

Nonfiction

Areas	Possible Sources
what to do	teachers
	good students
	poor students
bad grade	counselors (What is a bad grade?)
	teachers (What is a bad grade?)
	survey of student opinion

Fiction

Areas	Possible Sources
crash	a pilot
plane	a book about airplanes
Amazon	a film-strip about the Amazon
fight	book on survival
jungle	a jungle exhibit at the zoo
small town	map of Brazil

Step 4: Make a notebook and choose priorities.

Research takes time. You may run out of time for researching, so you will want to cover the most important areas first and the least important areas last.

Make a little notebook with one page for each area. Write the area, your pointers, and your sources at the top of the page. You can use the bottom of the page for taking notes. Arrange your notebook pages in order of importance. You can staple your pages together after you have them in order, or put them in a three-ring binder.

Now you are ready to research. Your notebook reminds you what to research, in what order, and whom to ask or where to look. Be sure to make a note of which books you actually read and which experts you actually consult. Sources don't always work out like you might expect. You'll need to adjust your sources depending on who or what you find while you are researching.

Activity 5:
Finding Expert Sources

∾ Everybody is ignorant, only on different
subjects.

—Will Rogers

Everyone is an "expert" to a writer. It's just a matter of discovering the subject. Hang around writers on their daily rounds and you'll find them asking the store clerk how the new shoes are working out, debating menu changes with the owner of the local café, and sympathizing with the bus driver over schedule changes. Bums will not get a quarter from a writer without first explaining the best place to sleep on the streets. After all, writing after library research is not the same as writing after discussing the subject with an expert source.

The students, families, and teachers of the average class form a vast pool of experts, who have traveled to all corners of the globe, learned to speak several languages, built everything from log canoes to high-rises, done every job from lumberjack to politician. They know how to grade diamonds and make soda pop, and they have lived through wars, fires, tornadoes, depressions, and floods.

For students, interviewing an expert source makes writing twice as much fun. We use this class project to create a class file of homegrown experts who are willing to be interviewed by students during the school year. Making the file gives students valuable experience with interviewing and an entirely different view of the so-called average people around them.

Before you begin, prepare copies of the "Class Experts Questionnaire" and the "Outside Experts Questionnaire" and warn your fellow teachers that they are about to be pestered by writing students with a bunch of personal questions. (For younger students, you may also want to type an explanatory letter that they can take with them.) Pair students together in interview teams. It's much easier to overcome sudden attacks of shyness, to remember what to ask, and to record the answers with two interviewers.

Choose a convenient method for filing and cross-referencing the written interviews by name and area of expertise.

Instructions to Students

Experts are all around you. Consulting one may not be as hard as you think. The "Expert Sources File" is a class project. What we need is a list of people who are willing to talk to students. We also need to learn each person's areas of expertise. Once we have the file, members of the class can use it to locate expert sources when they write research strategies.

Everyone you know is an expert on something. Perhaps one of the teachers in this school used to be a professional rodeo cowboy. Perhaps another works on an archeological dig in England every summer. Another might collect precious stones. One of your parents might run an ice cream factory, another might be a secretary for a big corporation, and still another might work at city hall. These people are experts. Rodeos, archeology, precious stones, ice cream, big corporations, and city hall are their areas of expertise. When you write stories, you might want to research one of these areas by talking with an expert source.

How do you find out what a person's area of expertise is? You ask them questions; for example, "What jobs have you held?" When one of them says "rodeo cowboy," you know that this person could be an expert for a student writing a story that has a rodeo scene. A person might be an expert in more than one area. That's what you are going to do for this project: ask people questions and find out their areas of expertise.

To do this project, you will work with another student and interview at least two people you know. Once you have completed an interview, you will fill in the blanks at the top of your interview questionnaire with a list of the person's areas of expertise.

In-Class Experts

The experts we know best are ourselves. How many of you have lived in another town? Have gone to another school? Have a hobby outside school? Know about something that the rest of the class might not know about? Fill out the "Class Experts Questionnaire" for our file of expert sources.

Don't think that you need a Ph.D. in an important field to be an expert. Your fellow classmates may need to know about little things, too. If you collect stamps or raise ants, write it down. Some mystery writers may need to know about stamps; some science fiction writers may need to know about ants.

We've left space at the bottom of the questionnaire. If you think of a good question to ask your fellow students, come write it on the chalkboard. Use the space at the bottom of your questionnaires to answer any of the questions on the chalkboard. (Note: We always get the chalkboard questions started by writing, "What's the hardest thing you've ever had to do?")

Outside Experts

You don't need to go very far to find outside experts. Besides your fellow students, you can also use teachers, parents, and neighbors as experts. Don't forget grandparents, aunts, and uncles who live nearby. When you first talk to an outside expert, explain what you are doing. First, ask them if would be willing to be interviewed by students who are researching stories. If they say "No," thank them and choose another person. If your expert source says "Yes," explain that you are interviewing people who might have some special expertise that they could share.

(Text continues on p. 48.)

Class Experts Questionnaire

<u>Student Handout</u>
(Fill in areas of expertise after the interview.)

Areas of expertise:

_____   _____

_____   _____

_____   _____

Name (first and last): _____ .

Best day and time for interview: _____ .

Home room number and teacher: _____ .

1. Have you ever lived in another town? Where? How long ago did you live there? How old were you when you lived there?

2. Do you know any languages other than English?

3. Is anyone in your family from another town? Another country?

4. What's your favorite subject in school? Have you ever done anything outside school related to your favorite subject?

5. Name three of your hobbies outside school.

6. What are the most interesting places you've been on vacation?

7. Do you belong to any organizations outside school, such as the Scouts, a karate club, a ham radio club, a "young astronauts" club, or a band? List them.

8. Have you written enough about a particular area that you think you could help others in the class who don't know about it?

9. If you were another student in the class trying to find an expert, what areas would you ask yourself about?

Interviewed by: _____ Date: _____

Use the space below for answering questions from the chalkboard:

Outside Experts Questionnaire

<u>Student Handout</u>
(Fill in areas of expertise after the interview.)

Areas of expertise:

_____   _____

_____   _____

_____   _____

Name (first and last): _____

Best day and time for interview: _____

Address: _____

Telephone: _____

1. How do you spell your name?

2. When and where could a student contact you?

3. If students writing stories or magazine articles need to talk with an "expert," what subjects do you think you could help them with?

4. What is your job?

5. Have you held other jobs that students might want to ask you about?

6. Do you have any special hobbies?

7. Have you ever built anything?

8. Have you ever learned to fix anything; for example, cars or household appliances?

9. Have you ever lived anywhere besides here? Where?

(Note to interviewer: Be sure to say "Thank you.")

Interviewed by: _____ Date: _____

Activity 6:
Giving Your Characters
a Background

～ The characters have their own lives and their
own logic and you have to act accordingly.

—Isaac Bashevis Singer

Students often assume that the name makes the character, even though their main characters are completely "flat." This activity helps fiction students get to know some of the things that make a character "round." Students enjoy talking to their imaginary characters and often want to keep writing, so allow plenty of time.

Instructions to Students

Whatever happens in your story happens because of a character. Your characters act or react to something. They act or react because of their background: their previous experiences, their opinions, and their personalities. Characters are just like real people. They have names, live somewhere, hold jobs, go to school, own pets, and have pet peeves. They even get tired and cranky.

Part of the fiction writer's background research is getting to know the characters. It's easy to do—just ask your characters some questions. The "Interview with a Character" handout provides a list of questions directed toward the character. Work with another student in the class: One of you asks the questions while the other pretends to be a character from his or her story and answers the questions. Don't forget to write down the answers. When you have finished the interview, whoever was the interviewer pretends to be a character while the other asks the questions.

Interview with a Character

<u>Student Handout</u>

1. Are you the main character in the story or a secondary character?

2. What is your full name (first, middle, and last)?

3. Do you have a nickname? What is it? How did you get that nickname?

4. How does your name fit your personality? Do you like your name? Even your middle name?

5. How old are you? What year were you born?

6. Where do you live? Do you live alone or with other people? Who lives with you? Are the people you live with characters in the story?

7. Do you have a job? What is it? Where do you work? What are the hours? How long have you done that job? What did you do before? Do you like your job?

8. Do you go to school? What grade? What's your best subject? What's your worst? Do you like school?

9. How tall are you? What build (thin, medium, heavy, etc.)? How much do you weigh? What color is your hair? Your eyes?

10. Are you rich, poor, or average? Does it matter to you whether or not you have money?

11. Which three of the following traits best describe you:

angry	detached	good-natured	messy	shy
artistic	dreamer	graceful	neat	snobbish
bold	dull	hard-working	organized	sympathetic
bubbly	energetic	imaginative	outgoing	tense
careful	enthusiastic	intellectual	powerful	thoughtful
cheerful	frantic	intelligent	practical	tight-fisted
clumsy	frustrated	lazy	quiet	timid
confused	funny	lonely	realistic	tough
critical	fussy	loud	relaxed	unhappy
curious	generous	loyal	serious	worried

12. What would you most like to have?

13. What is your biggest pet peeve?

14. What do other people always tell you about yourself?

15. What is the best thing about you? The worst?

16. When are you happiest?

17. Choose any three of your answers and write two or three paragraphs explaining those answers.

Activity 7:
Making a Pictionary

> Thought itself needs words. It runs on them
> like beads on a string.
>
> —Ugo Betti

The old tradition of handing out a list of vocabulary words for students to use in their stories doesn't work when every student is writing a different piece. It's just as well. The vocabulary never helped that much anyway. It's hard enough to think of a story without having to use certain words to tell it.

Making a pictionary is fun, but more important, it helps students collect vocabulary related to their pieces. It's easy to do: Draw a picture of the subject, setting, characters, or anything else related to the piece and label all the components of the picture with words. Students can use a professional pictionary, such as a *What's What* (try the one by Reginald Bregonier and David Fisher) to look up more words for their pictures. For the inartistic, "stick" pictures on notebook paper work as well as fancy drawings. For the artistic, this activity may peak their interest in writing.

Instructions to Students

What's a pictionary? It's a dictionary of pictures that includes all the words for every-thing in the pictures. Making a pictionary helps you write because you learn words you need for your story before you begin. Making a pictionary is simple. Draw a picture of something in your story: the subject, your characters, or the setting. Label everything in the picture with words. Make a list of all the words in the picture below your drawing.

There is a book on the reference shelf called *What's What*. It's a pictionary, too, about all sorts of subjects. You can look in it for ideas of more words you might need for your story and add them to your list. If you don't know how to spell a word, look up the correct spelling before you write it in your pictionary. This is a good place to use *The Misspeller's Dictionary*, which lists words by common misspellings.

EXAMPLE

Pictionary 1.

EXAMPLE

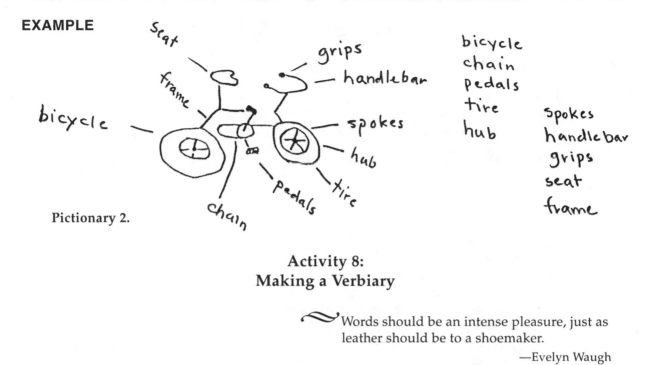

Pictionary 2.

bicycle
chain
pedals
tire
hub

spokes
handlebar
grips
seat
frame

Activity 8:
Making a Verbiary

∽ Words should be an intense pleasure, just as leather should be to a shoemaker.

—Evelyn Waugh

A good rule of style is: Never use an adverb when a good strong verb will do. Verbs are the heart of the English sentence. The language makes up for its weak conjugation by a flexible use of verbs and a big vocabulary of verbs. A good vocabulary of verbs is the most important vocabulary for students to develop.

Making a verbiary helps students list verbs they can use, but more important, it imitates what they must do to think of verbs when they are writing. Although it's good practice, making a verbiary is not an easy exercise. Show students how to do it before they begin, and circulate from table to table to help fill in any missing vocabulary.

Depending on the sophistication of the class, this exercise may provide an opportunity to discuss how English verbs work. For example, students may encounter verb phrases where another word becomes an essential part of the verb. "Famine drove up the price of wheat" and "The tour bus drove up the road" both use "up" as part of the verb, and the verb phrase has two different meanings, just as a single verb may have. Even if you don't discuss verbs in this fine detail, have students list both the verb and the verb phrase on their lists. This will become important later when they begin using the lists to look up synonyms for the verbs.

Instructions to Students

In case you've forgotten, nouns are the words for people, places, and things. Verbs are the action of a sentence. They are what those people, places, and things do—even if they just sit there. In the sentence "The dog jumped over the house," *dog* is a noun and *jumped* is a verb.

Look at the list of words from your pictionary. Most of them are nouns, aren't they? Today we're going to make a verbiary to go with your pictionary, just to make sure you've got plenty of verbs on hand for your story.

Sit with your writing groups today. We'll show you how to do this once before you try it on your own. The handout will help you remember the steps.

Making a Verbiary

<u>Student Handout</u>

Step 1: Find some verbs.

Write a list of just the nouns in your pictionary down the left-hand side of a sheet of paper. Next to each, write a simple sentence using that noun. Draw a line under the verb in your sentences.

EXAMPLE

peak—The man <u>climbed</u> the peak.
mountain—The mountain <u>turned</u> purple.
cloud—The cloud <u>rained</u>.
forest—The forest <u>swayed</u> in the wind.
road—The family <u>drove</u> up the road.
car—The car <u>broke</u> <u>down</u>.
stream—The stream <u>flowed</u> down the mountain.

Step 2: Make a list of verbs.

You now have a list of sentences with the verbs underlined. On a separate sheet of paper, make a list of just the verbs. Next to each verb, write one of the following adverbs: *quickly, slowly, angrily, suddenly, happily, sadly.*

EXAMPLE

climbed quickly	drove angrily
turned angrily	broke slowly
rained happily	flowed sadly
swayed quickly	

Step 3: Brainstorm to find new verbs.

With your writing group, try to think of a verb for each verb-adverb pair that says the same thing. List the new verbs. You may not be able to think of a verb for everything. You can look up the verb in the thesaurus or synonym finder to see if there is a word that means something close to "climbed quickly" or "turned angrily" and so forth.

EXAMPLE

climbed quickly	ran	turned angrily	glared
	clambered		scowled
	dashed		frowned
	floated up	broke slowly	disintegrated
	shot up		crumbled
	danced		fell apart
			decomposed

From *Teaching Writing in Middle School.* © 1998 Beth Means and Lindy Lindner. Teacher Ideas Press. (800) 237-6124.

Activity 9:
Making a Word-Finder

> ❧ [Words] . . . can change their meanings right
> in front of you. They pick up flavors and
> odors like butter in a refrigerator.
>
> —John Steinbeck

Students are fascinated with synonyms. Few things increase their vocabulary faster than browsing through a thesaurus finding synonyms and antonyms for words they already know. Making a word-finder based on words likely to appear in their writing provides them with a ready reference they understand (because they made it themselves), and it gives them a sense of power over the words in their story.

You'll need ten or fifteen copies of dictionaries appropriate for students and about the same number of paperback thesauri. If you can afford several copies of J. I. Rodale's *The Synonym Finder* (it's expensive), have them available, too. We prefer *The Synonym Finder* to a thesaurus because it has many more synonyms and, unlike the thesaurus, it arranges synonyms by definition.

Tell students that they will need a pencil, their pictionary and verbiary lists (or any other vocabulary list), a package of 3-by-5-inch index cards, a rubber band, and a folder for storing the cards. (We normally avoid using index cards, but they work well for making word-finders.)

Students need help learning to use the reference works. Model the activity once for the class, and use the "Making a Word-Finder" handout to help them remember the steps (or use an overhead transparency or the chalkboard). As students make their word-finders, wander around the classroom to offer help. This activity takes time, but per pound of vocabulary learned, it's a real time-saver.

Instructions to Students

There are about 600,000 words in the English language, and we want you to learn them all by Friday. Just kidding. We do want to talk to you about words. The English language has more words than any other language in the world. This makes it a wonderful language for writing; there's always a perfect word sitting out there—you just have to find it. The more words you know, the easier it is to write. One of the things you should try to do before you begin to write is expand your vocabulary.

Your vocabulary is all the words you know. You'll be amazed to learn how many words you already know—maybe 3,000 by the time you reach age twelve. You learn about 1,000 words a year without even trying, but you can speed the process by making word-finders before you write. To make a word-finder, you begin with the list of words you know from making your pictionaries and verbiaries. Then you look in a synonym-finder or a thesaurus and gather more words.

The words you will be gathering are called synonyms and antonyms. A synonym is a word that means the same thing as another word. An antonym is a word that means the opposite. You may wonder why we have synonyms. Well, synonyms mean the same thing, but not exactly the same thing. For example, some synonyms for the word *blue* are *turquoise*, *azure*, *navy*, *baby-blue*, *sapphire*, and *aquamarine*. They all mean "blue," but different shades of blue. Synonyms are words that mean the same thing, but they have different shades of meaning.

There is another important feature of words. The same word can mean two things. *Blue* can mean "the color blue" or it can mean "sad," as in "I'm feeling blue today." So other synonyms for *blue* are *glum, unhappy, morose, dismal, bleak*, and *depressed*.

Antonyms are words that mean the opposite. There isn't any "opposite" for the color blue, but there are opposites for the "sad" kind of blue: *happy, delighted, cheerful, cheery, sunny*, and *positive*.

Today you will be making word-finders—lists of synonyms and antonyms that you might want to use in your stories. Sit with your writing groups. We've put a dictionary and a synonym-finder or thesaurus on each table. You'll need your lists of pictionary and verbiary words and 3-by-5-inch index cards.

Always make word-finders using a pencil, so you can erase. You can work alone or as a group, taking turns. The handout has instructions and examples. When you have finished, put your cards in alphabetical order, put a rubber band around them, and store them in a folder so that you don't lose them.

(Text continues on p. 57.)

Making a Word-Finder

<u>Student Handout</u>

Reminders:

 ◆ Synonyms are words that have nearly the same meaning, but with slightly different shades of meaning.

 ◆ Antonyms are words that have the opposite meaning.

 ◆ A dictionary lists words alphabetically and explains what they mean. Words often have more than one meaning. Each new meaning of a word is numbered.

EXAMPLE

 blue
 1. a color
 2. sad or unhappy

 ◆ A synonym-finder lists words alphabetically, followed by synonyms for each word. Each numbered group of synonyms represents synonyms for a particular meaning of the word.

EXAMPLE

 blue
 1. turquoise, azure, navy, baby-blue, sapphire, aquamarine
 2. glum, unhappy, morose, dismal, bleak, depressed

 ◆ A thesaurus is like a synonym-finder, but it lists synonyms and antonyms, and it doesn't divide them by meaning like the synonym-finder.

EXAMPLE

 blue

 syn.—turquoise, azure, navy, baby-blue, sapphire, aquamarine, glum, unhappy, morose, dismal, bleak, depressed

 ant.—happy, delighted, cheerful, cheery, sunny, positive

There are three steps to making a word-finder:

Step 1: Set up your index cards.

Choose a word from your pictionary or verbiary list. Write it in big letters at the top of the index card. Make one card for each of the words from your pictionary and verbiary.

Step 2: Check the spelling and meaning in the dictionary.

Look up each word in the dictionary. Check the spelling on your card. Correct the spelling if necessary. Read the definitions, so that you know what other meanings your word might have.

Step 3: Find synonyms and antonyms.

Look up each word in the thesaurus or synonym-finder. Read the list of synonyms. These will be listed next to the abbreviation *syn*. Choose at least four synonyms that you like. (Don't necessarily choose the first four. Choose short, punchy synonyms that you like.) Write "syn." on the front of your index card and then write the synonyms you have chosen. Check the spelling.

If you are using a thesaurus: Antonyms will be listed next to the abbreviation *ant*. Choose at least three antonyms that you like. Turn your index card over, write "ant." at the top, and write the antonyms you have chosen. Check the spelling.

If you are using a synonym-finder: A synonym-finder only lists synonyms, so you must think of an antonym, then look up that word in the synonym-finder. Choose at least three antonyms that you like. Turn your index card over, write "ant." at the top, and write the antonyms you have chosen. Check the spelling.

EXAMPLE

(front of card)

```
PEAK
syn.

summit, crest, ridge, mountain-
top, cliff, tip, cap, spire
```

(back of card)

```
ant.

valley, depression, ravine, gully,
river basin
```

Step 4: Arrange cards alphabetically.

Arrange your word-finder cards in alphabetical order, put a rubber band around them, and store them in a folder.

PART 3:
FINDING AN ORDER

Writing is thinking on paper, but trying to draft and think simultaneously is difficult. Unlike thinking, writing is both linear and sequential; that is, it must be done one word at a time in a certain order. Thoughts, however, do not arrive one at a time in a particular sequence. They come in patterns and seem to choose their own time, arriving at inconvenient moments and disappearing when they are needed.

A prewriting outline is not really an attempt to organize the writing. That can only be done—well—during revision. When writers outline, they are attempting to remove the pressure to write and think simultaneously by handling some of the thinking ahead of time. They need to use outlining methods suited to that task.

To most teachers and their students, the word *outline* means the traditional topic outline:

   I. First Main Topic
      A. Subtopic
      B. Subtopic
         1. Sub-subtopic
         2. Sub-subtopic
  II. Second Main Topic
      A. Subtopic
      B. Subtopic

(Remember, if you include subtopics, you must have at least two; if you include sub-subtopics, you must have at least two.)

Although you should introduce your students to the topic outline (if they aren't already familiar with it), bear in mind its disadvantages, especially for beginning writers. Instead of helping the writer think through some of the relationships between ideas before writing about them, the topic outline attempts to classify and subordinate ideas. Ideas are not so docile: They declare independence in the middle of a draft. Minor point II.C.4 turns into a monster and chews up the first main topic while the second main topic steadfastly insists on becoming a footnote. Then what?

If you want students to outline, try abandoning the topic outline and substituting a variety of outlining methods that help them collect their ideas before they begin to write. Almost any method that serves one or more of the following purposes will do:

  1. To collect facts and ideas in one place

  2. To break the piece into scenes or sections that can be written one at a time

  3. To organize ideas and information for easy retrieval

Choosing a genre with a built-in sense of order is the simplest form of outlining. How-to, tips, questions and answers, and "a day in the life" all work well. Outlines do not need to be made before drafting; the first draft itself can serve as a useful outline. Outlining with scissors and tape is a time-honored tradition among writers. With word-processing software to reduce some of the pain, cut and paste is gaining popularity. Branching, design, and the other alternatives covered in this part are all simple ways to replace the topic outline.

Whatever method students choose, don't overdo outlining. Many students do not have enough experience with writing to be able to anticipate it with an outline, and some people never can outline without first putting words on paper.

Activity 10:
Branching

> 〜 One of the only virtues of linear outlining
> is that it looks neat, and that very virtue is
> its downfall. By working hard to make sure
> the outline is neat, we effectively cut off any
> additions and insertions, any new idea.
>
> —Henriette Klauser

Branching is one of the best outlining methods for thinking ideas through quickly and recording thoughts before they disappear. Its other virtue is that it produces a visible picture of the entire piece, so that students can begin to see where they are going.

This method was invented by Tony Buzan as a reading comprehension tool, but it is just as useful for brainstorming, outlining, or almost any other kind of planning. If you want more details on the method, see Buzan's book, *Use Both Sides of Your Brain*, which uses a branching method called mind-mapping; primarily used as a reading comprehension and study tool, or Henriette Anne Klauser's *Writing on Both Sides of the Brain*, which has an extensive discussion of branching.

Instructions to Students

You can make writing easier if you take some time before you begin writing to explore your ideas of what you might write. One easy way to do this is to make a branching outline.

EXAMPLE

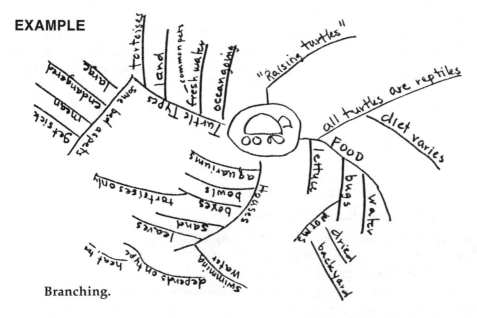

Branching.

To make this branch, we began with our writing idea at the center and drew a picture of a turtle just for fun. We could have used the word *turtle* instead. The first thing we thought of was the title, "Raising Turtles." The next idea we had was that turtles need food, so we drew a branch for "Food" and collected our ideas about turtle food on little branches shooting off the "Food" branch. The idea of food suggested houses, so we made a branch for "Houses" and collected our ideas about turtle houses. We collected all our ideas, no matter how trivial or silly they sounded. If we weren't sure about a fact, we just wrote a question mark after it.

We want you to try making a branch outline of your current story or nonfiction piece. There are not really any rules to follow, but here are some things to keep in mind:

- Begin at the center of the paper with a picture or a word representing your writing idea or some part of your writing idea.

- It is perfectly okay to be messy, to draw little pictures, to use colored pens, to use big pieces of paper, or to do something else. Don't try to be too pretty about it because that might slow you down. You want to collect your ideas as fast as you can. You can always draw a tidy branch later.

- Remember that ideas come in waves. If you run out of ideas, keep drawing branches and trying to fill them in until the next wave comes. Always try to branch for at least ten minutes, so that you catch more than one wave of ideas.

- You don't need to work on one branch until you finish it. If an idea for another branch comes to mind, work awhile on that branch.

- Record all your ideas, no matter how trivial or silly they seem at first. You can decide which ones to use later.

- Have fun! You'll be surprised by how much you know.

Activity 11:
The Design

> ∾ To be simple is the best thing in the world; to be modest is the next best thing. I am not so sure about being quiet.
>
> —G. K. Chesterton

Underlying most good nonfiction is a very simple design. Designs either break a nonfiction piece into manageable sections or suggest an order of presentation. Having some idea what those designs are helps many students begin to organize nonfiction.

You should not try to teach designs as an activity. Just pass out the "Designs" handout and tell students that they can use a design to help them outline. Design will soon pop up in students' work.

Instructions to Students

All nonfiction must have a simple plan, a logic behind the writing. This is not a complex outline, just a simple design. The writer makes up the design. It can be any design that the writer thinks will work. You can choose a design for your nonfiction piece, then use the design to help you write your outline. There are a thousand different designs. In the "Designs" handout are some ideas for different types of designs you might want to use.

Designs

<u>Student Handout</u>

Sequential Design

This design is based on the order in which something is done or something took place. For example, a how-to article explains what to do first, second, and third in the order the reader is supposed to do them.

Past-Present-Future

This is a popular design in which the writer reviews what happened in the past, what's happening now, and what is likely to happen in the future. Examples can be found in most science magazines, such as *Omni*. Lincoln's "Gettysburg Address" is another good example.

Most Important Point to Least Important Point
(or Least Important to Most Important)

This design is most often used to make a case for a key idea. For example, if you are writing a movie review, your key idea may be that the movie was bad. Using this design, you would first list the most important reason it was bad, then the next most important reason it was bad, and so forth, and finish with the least important reason (or vice versa).

Specific to General (or General to Specific)

This design begins with specific facts or examples and moves to more general statements (or vice versa). For example, if you are explaining how to fly a hot-air balloon, you could tell the specific story of how one person does it and then show how this person's method follows general rules for flying. Or, first explain the general rules for flying hot-air balloons and then give specific examples of one person doing it, to illustrate those rules.

Three Balanced Points

This is the classic design of the traditional essay or report. The writer chooses at least three (and up to five) points to make about the key idea and expands each point equally. The writer also includes an introduction and a conclusion.

Storyplan

This design is written like a fictional story but concludes by making a point. For example, you could tell the story of flying a hot-air balloon and then conclude by discussing why people like the sport.

Musical Design

This design is often used for speeches. Repetition of phrases or words carry the plan, so the speech sounds almost musical. One of the masters of this design was Martin Luther King, Jr.—his "I Have a Dream" speech is a good example.

Activity 12:
Outlining Alternatives

∼ He thinks things through very clearly before going off half-cocked.

—General Carl Spatz

The number of outlining methods is limited only by the imagination.[1] We use this activity to encourage students to try some other methods of outlining besides branching and design. Point out to students that different methods of outlining serve different purposes. They may want to make two or more outlines. The point is to create an outline that makes drafting the piece easier.

Instructions to Students

Writing a story or a nonfiction piece is an adventure, like taking a trip. Have you ever watched people plan for trips? They are very funny about it. Fenton Quagmire plans his trip by packing everything in the car he might possibly need, including a lot of junk he will never use. He buys maps of everything and tries to plan every step of the trip in little red lines. Betty Blastoff takes off with a dollar in her pocket and a box of corn flakes. She makes up the trip as she goes along.

Planning a piece of writing is just like planning for a trip. The outline is the place you store your maps and anything else you might need along the way. Like Fenton, you can pack every little thing you might need into an outline, or you can blast off like Betty and make it up as you go along. Fenton and Betty are extremes. You may want to plan something between the extremes. Do enough planning to decide the major points, but make up the details as you write. Here's a good rule of thumb to keep in mind: Any time you blast off without a plan, plan to do more editing than usual.

There are many different methods of outlining. We've already shown you branching and design. Today we have a handout with some other outlining methods. You can use whichever method helps you the most. Remember, the only reason for making an outline is to make drafting easier. You can include anything in your outline you think will help.

(Text continues on p. 65.)

---

1. If you want more outlining ideas, Donald M. Murray has tucked a comprehensive treasury of outlining methods in the middle of his wonderful book, *A Writer Teaches Writing* (a book all writing teachers should read).

Outlining Methods

Student Handout

Collection Boxes

For this method of outlining, divide the piece into several major categories, then collect your facts and ideas under each category.

EXAMPLE

Key Idea

Owning a pet turtle

Category 1: Feeding Habits

Likes leafy vegetables and bugs or worms

Prepared foods at pet store

Category 2: Types of Turtles

Box turtles, common green turtles are swimming turtles

Terrapins are land turtles

Swimming turtles need more care than land turtles

Category 3: Where to Get Turtles

Pet stores

Veterinarians (sometimes get pets people don't want)

Zoo might have information

In the wild (only common types, not endangered)

Fiction writers might use categories such as settings, characters, and scene ideas. The purpose of making a collection is to store information and ideas where they are easy to find. It is especially useful when you have a lot of background research you will need to review as you write.

Critical Pieces

To make this type of outline, write certain critical scenes or sections first, then fill in the outline using one of the other outlining methods. For example, you could write the conclusion, then use branching, design, or collection to outline the rest of the piece. Fiction writers might write the scene with the climax or the ending, then fill in events that happened before that scene.

The Slugline

Newspaper reporters write the stories, but somebody else writes the titles, or headlines, for the stories. The printers use a temporary headline, called a slug, to keep track of a story that doesn't yet have a title. A slug describes the story in no more than five words. "Man Bites Dog" is the classic example of a slug. It tells an entire story in just three words. You can plan your pieces or stories with slugs. Write one slug for the overall piece or story, then write slugs for each major section or scene.

EXAMPLE

Overall: Turtles as Pets

Section 1: Buying a Turtle

Section 2: Making Your Turtle a Home

Section 3: Feeding Your Turtle

Sketching

When artists plan a big painting, they do practice sketches of little parts of the painting first. You can plan your writing with practice sketches.

EXAMPLES

Fiction

- Describe your main character walking down a hall, getting mad about something, talking with a friend, talking with a stranger, being frightened by something, or feeling enthusiastic about something.

- Describe a character looking at the setting of the story.

Nonfiction

- Pick any idea in your piece and think about it from two points of view. Explain why you agree with the idea, then explain why you disagree with the idea.

- Write a letter to your ideal reader explaining why he or she needs to read what you are going to write.

- Write a letter to your writing group explaining how you plan to organize your piece and why.

- What is the most important idea or piece of information you intend to write about? Why is it more important than some of the other ideas?

- Choose any idea, fact, or instruction in your piece and write an example.

Chaining

Write one paragraph of your piece. Choose one sentence from that paragraph to use as the first sentence of your next paragraph. Write a paragraph about that sentence. Keep chaining one paragraph to another until you have four or five paragraphs, then cross out the repeated sentences.

From *Teaching Writing in Middle School.* © 1998 Beth Means and Lindy Lindner. Teacher Ideas Press. (800) 237-6124.

Chaining is fun to do with a friend. You write the first paragraph, your friend chains on the next one, you write the third, and so forth.

EXAMPLE

> Peanut butter and jelly sandwiches are good, but they are hard to make. The peanut butter rips up the bread, and the jelly dribbles out the edges and sticks to everything. The first time you make a peanut butter and jelly sandwich, keep a wet washrag close by. If you go slowly, you won't make a mess.
>
> *The peanut butter rips up the bread, and jelly dribbles out the edges and sticks to everything.* Peanut butter is made of ground-up peanuts. If the peanuts don't contain very much oil, the peanut butter doesn't flow onto the sandwich as well. Jelly, however, is mostly made of sugar and water. The water makes it flow out of the sandwich, and the sugar makes it sticky.

Cut and Paste

Sometimes, it's easiest to just get your ideas written down while they are fresh, then organize them later. With this outlining method, you outline after you write a rough draft. First, write a rough draft of the entire piece from beginning to end. Then cut apart sentences and paragraphs and tape them together in a new order. Finally, fill in any missing sentences or rewrite sentences that don't fit. You can use a design or any other outlining method to help you decide how to put together your cut-up piece.

Mixed Method

You can mix and match your outlining methods. For example, you could break your story into major sections with sluglines, and then record all your ideas for that section with a branch.

TEACHER'S NOTEBOOK

On Writing Groups and Writing Conferences

Writing is a solo occupation, but writers still need friends with whom to share the process. Traditionally, they form writing groups to meet regularly and share work-in-progress. Students, too, can benefit from a writing group. At the beginning of the school year or term, divide the class into writing groups of three to four students each. Keep students together in their writing groups for the entire year or term. With younger students start with pairs and work up to groups after they have learned to get work done in pairs.

The writing group should be responsible for helping every student in the group. Members of the group should be encouraged to serve as a sounding-board for ideas, as assistants when the going gets rough, and as editors. Before students bring problems to the teacher, they should check with their writing group first. If the group cannot solve the problem, students may then make an appointment with the teacher.

Students do find talking over problems with the teacher reassuring. Try setting up a formal conference system, as Donald H. Graves suggests in *Writing: Teachers and Children at Work*. Students or entire writing groups can make appointments for a writing conference with the teacher during drafting or editing sessions. The appointment is important. It assures students that they will get a chance to talk with the teacher and also delays the conference just a little, so they might solve their problems themselves while they wait.

Graves also suggests that teachers conduct conferences with predictable steps:

1. Ask, "How can I help you?"

2. Let students try to express what is bothering them.

3. Read sections of their work aloud.

4. Discuss possible options and leave the decision to the student.

Keep the conference short, not more than five minutes.

On Writing Terms

Knowing a little jargon gives students a big boost. When they learn terms such as *character*, *fiction*, and *ideal reader*, they learn more about the choices they can make, and they have some way to talk about their

writing. Just knowing that there are such things as *genres*, *settings*, *dialogue*, *action*, and *examples* inspires writing. Understanding what a *scene* is or what a *section* is helps them organize their work.

Teaching writing necessarily involves teaching terminology, but there are some significant problems with teaching writing jargon. First of all, writing terms are vague and don't hold up to precise definition. Most represent a decision made by writers, for good or ill. A *sentence* is anything the writer begins with a capital letter and ends with a period. It's impossible to be more specific. Not all sentences have a subject and a verb or represent a unified thought. Even run-on and incomplete sentences are still sentences.

Secondly, no two writers, teachers, or editors use the same terms. They might call the *ideal reader* the *audience*, the *reader*, or the *market*. They might call the *key idea* the *slant*, *angle*, *purpose*, *topic*, *subject*, *narrowed topic* or *narrowed subject*, or the *lead*.

Finally, fiction and nonfiction writers need to know different terms. Critics use overlapping terms with a different emphasis. Discussing grammar or punctuation requires a set of terms aimed at dissecting sentences, useful only in the final stages of polishing.

Some writing teachers don't formally teach terms. They bring them up naturally during editing sessions and class discussion. Students gradually learn some terms by themselves. We prefer to hand our students a few vital terms on a platter, so that the group has some common base from which to begin discussing writing. Then we let the terminology flow from the activities.

By the end of a semester or so, we like our students to know *categories* and *genres*, the *prewriting choices*, *scenes* and *sections*, and at least some of the techniques from Chapters 4 and 5, such as *action*, *dialogue*, *examples*, and *anecdotes*. We teach grammar and punctuation separate from writing.

To overcome the circular definition problem while still giving students the terms at the outset, we use the same steps to teach every important term:

1. Define the term briefly and read aloud several examples to the group.

2. Ask students to try it in their practice journal (three to five minutes at most).

3. Ask volunteers to share practice pieces with the group.

4. Pass out some kind of follow-up literature. We like handouts for important terms or lists of suggestions because students can refer to them later. Summaries on the chalkboard or an overhead transparency are fine for transient terminology questions.

On Scenes and Sections

Outlines help everyone but the beginner. The major purpose of outlining is to break a piece of writing into smaller components (fiction *scenes* and nonfiction *sections*—see Chapters 4 and 5, respectively). Experienced writers can imagine what might happen in various scenes or sections as they outline. They can then use the outline to juggle the pieces into a sensible plan without a lot of rewriting. Beginners, however, have no idea what a scene or section might include until they write it. For them, outlining is like trying to put together a puzzle without any pieces. There are two completely separate writing skills involved: 1) writing solid fictional scenes or nonfiction sections in depth and 2) fitting together several scenes or sections. To effectively outline, students need experience with both.

Young students don't have the patience or stamina to learn both skills in one assignment. Students writing complete pieces, however short, do not learn to write in depth. Instead of outlining, try jumping directly into isolated scenes and sections with your students (see Chapters 4 and 5). Once students feel confident with scenes and sections, outlines make more sense. Teach students how to write isolated scenes and sections first; work toward writing complete pieces as they gain confidence and skill.

On Storing Papers

Lost papers cause hysteria in writing classrooms. Research notes and rough drafts soon create a blizzard of paper, much of it easily mistaken for scratch paper. The easiest way to solve the problem is to buy two cardboard banker's boxes: one for loose papers and one for portfolio pieces. Label two manila folders per student, one for each box.

Insist that students keep all their loose papers and their practice journals in their folders. Keep the box of student folders where students can retrieve whatever papers they need, without asking. School lockers seem to eat stories for lunch, so it may be easiest to have students leave everything in the box during the day and pick up anything they need for homework on the way home. A few will forget to come by after school, but that's a smaller crisis than a lost story.

Store clean, unmarked copies of portfolio pieces in folders in the portfolio box, under lock and key. Keep them until the end of the year, then return the entire folder. Students are thrilled to see all the work they did in a year. In the meantime, you'll have clean copies readily at hand for any publishing projects you have in mind. (See also "Teachers' Notebook: On Personal, Practice, and Portfolio Assignments," Chapter 1, and "Teacher's Notebook: On Simple Ways to Publish," Chapter 6.)

NOTES
FROM THE PROS

On Fair Play

The old proverb is "Teach the writer, not the writing." It's a good rule because writing doesn't always play fair. Despite enthusiasm and immense effort on the part of the writer, some pieces turn to spaghetti. Some turn to sand and can't be remade. Some seem to write themselves. It's not always clear why one piece won't settle down on the page or collapses altogether, whereas others just flow. With writing, those who sweat most may achieve the poorest results. It isn't fair, but it is part of writing. Most writers have failed manuscripts languishing in the file cabinet.

Keep an eye on students. If one or two can't seem to make a piece work despite a long struggle, give them credit for their effort and a face-saving alternative. They've learned more than the others. Those who persist in the face of such disasters should always get credit for bravery. It's part of learning to fail and try again, and that's a big part of learning to write.

How Long Will It Take?

Students may be interested to know how long it takes a professional writer to write something. The man to consult is Lawrence Block. In addition to writing novels, he writes a column for *Writer's Digest* and teaches writing workshops. Block's book, *Writing the Novel from Plot to Print*, is the best we've run across and is one of the most practical, honest, and down-to-earth books about actually getting any book—not just the novel—written. We recommend it for serious high-school students and more mature middle-school students who want to write a book. (Be aware, however, that Block is also honest about how he paid his dues by writing porn novels and why writing and drinking don't mix.) He became interested in writers' work habits and surveyed them. According to Block, most professionals average four to five pages a day, not counting research and planning or final editing and copyediting. From start to finish, a book a year—including time off between books—is a good output for a professional. That works out to something like one page a day. (And then there's Isaac Asimov, who wrote fifty pages a day, but he was truly unique.) Students may want to take another look at their planning. How long is this *really* going to take?

Getting the Words to Flow on Paper

MEANS

Every nightmare (and even dogs have them) hints at the secret of imaginative power in the human mind. What the stalled or not-yet-started writer needs is some magic for getting in touch with himself, some key.

—John Gardner

INTRODUCTION

Writing down a telephone message, directions to a friend's house, or the answer to a question on a test is nothing like writing a unified story, essay, or report—any more than painting a house is the same as painting a landscape. Drafting a complete piece is a whole new world.

When beginning writers first encounter this new world, the change is a shock. Someone writing down a telephone message knows how long it will take to write the message down and has an idea of what the result will be. Those writing longer pieces soon discover that sometimes they are hot, sometimes stone cold. They cannot estimate whether a drafting session will go well, nor can they estimate how long it will take to finish a piece. They are haunted by a sense that the result could easily be an embarrassing catastrophe, despite their effort. Worse yet, they have trouble deciding how well it turned out once they have finished—but this is not a problem for students alone. Professional writers often remark that they don't know how a piece turned out, even though they have just reread it. Students may only have a vague sense that they have lost control. "I can't make my imagination work on time," wailed one student.

The rules are upside down in the new world. Puzzling out how to manage takes a long time, especially if no one mentions that it *is* a new world, with different rules. Trying to cope under pressure leads a surprising number of students to suffer from writing blocks at an early age. Some find writing so painful that they refuse to try anymore.

Avoiding Writing Blocks

The term *writer's block* brings to mind an agonized genius living in a cold sweat, unable to get one line on paper, not a seventh-grader who scrawls out a few careless paragraphs and tosses the work at the teacher, never wanting to see it again. The fully blocked writer is a rare phenomenon, but almost all those who write face a few garden-variety writing problems at one time or another:

1. They can't get started.
2. They can't find a voice for the piece, and it sounds stilted, phony, or cramped.
3. They write in painful fits and jerks.
4. They can only write occasionally.
5. They can't finish.

6. They suddenly lose confidence in their work.

7. They hit a wall about two-thirds of the way through the writing.

As editor and writer Gene Fowler said, "Writing is easy; all you do is sit staring at a blank sheet of paper until the drops of blood form on your forehead." This is no joke. These obstacles cause more writing failures for students than anything else encountered in writing. If students can't surmount them, all progress ends.

Writing isn't one task, but many tasks combined. Some tasks require creativity, others objectivity. Unfortunately, it is nearly impossible to be creative and objective at once. This conflict is the basic source of writing blocks. To help students separate conflicting writing tasks, we tell them that learning to write in the new world is like training two people to do different jobs. Writing will be much easier if students pretend that they have two people inside themselves, taking turns working on the piece.

This is not a new idea. There have always been two sides to writing—a creative side and an editorial side. One of the first writers to note the split nature of writing was Virgil. Through the centuries, writers have called the two sides of writing many things: the creator and the critic, the writer and the editor, the unconscious and the conscious, the right brain and the left brain. We call them the artist and the craftsman.[1]

The Artist's Job Description

The artist is in charge of imagination and drafting. Don't be confused by the term *artist* into thinking that we are only discussing fiction. The artist drafts snappy business letters, clear lab reports, thoughtful commentaries, and winning legal briefs, as well as riveting dialogue and vivid description. The artist supplies the basic materials of any written piece:

analogies	natural voice	sentences
ideas	observation	style
images	organizational unity	synthesis
individuality	paragraphs	unity of thought
metaphors	patterns	whimsy
mood	rhythm	word flow

Craftsman's Job Description

The craftsman—a sort of business manager for the artist—is in charge of organization and editing, and deals with the outside world. The craftsman

- ◆ decides when, where, and how long the artist will write;

- ◆ puts together plans;

---

1. Female craftsmen tell us that they still prefer the word *craftsman* to *craftswoman* or *craftsperson* because the substitutes sound so clumsy—the very thing good craftsmen are not. We bow to their choice, at least in part, because it provides a good opportunity for discussing with students the evolution of language.

- analyzes and judges the drafts;

- gives the artist suggestions for revision;

- finds the proper detail or word when the artist's choice isn't quite right;

- polishes and produces the final piece; and

- deals with teachers, editors, and readers.

Happily, there are just two ground rules for writing free of blocks:

1. Separate the artist from the craftsman.

    The key to writing free of blocks is to separate the work of the artist from the work of the craftsman, throughout the writing process. Each has a set of jobs. Don't mix them. For example, never mix drafting and editing. Drafting needs word flow—an artist's job. Editing, however, requires judgment—a craftsman's job.

    Spelling, punctuation, vocabulary, and penmanship are tools of the craftsman and should never be considered during early drafts. Concern about these details will slow down the drafting and break the artist's train of thought. Also, establishing the work conditions is the craftsman's job. When the artist does this, it's called daydreaming, not writing.

    Allow time between doing the tasks of the artist and doing those of the craftsman. For example, don't try to draft and edit in the same session. Don't even try to plan and draft in the same session. With experience, writers can learn to separate two tasks during the same session, but beginners should probably allow at least twenty-four hours between tasks.

    Once students learn the two sets of jobs, many like to give their personal artist and craftsman names to help keep them separate.

2. Give the artist and the craftsman equal standing and train them to equal strength.

    One is not "better" than the other. A weakness in one weakens both. If the craftsman becomes too strong, too critical, or interferes too soon, the artist is blocked. The words won't flow and there isn't much for the craftsman to prune and shape later. However, the artist can be lazy. Without the help of the craftsman, the writer may never finish. The artist and the craftsman must be equally strong, and must work together in harmony.

    There is an artist in each of us. To tap into our creative powers, we only need to know one thing: The artist is already there. One student called his artist The Force, tempting us to take the entire class to see *Star Wars*. Luke Skywalker finds his artist by finding The Force. He doesn't need to create The Force; he just needs to learn how to release it and then how to direct it. This is how writers train their artists.

The activities in this chapter belong to the artists in your students. In Part 1 are activities designed to help students release the artists within. In Part 2 are activities designed to help students direct their artists. Be prepared to have fun, and try to make drafting class as magical as you can. The artist thrives on magic.

PART 1:
FREEING THE ARTIST

All activities in this part should be done in a practice journal or on scratch paper so students will not be tempted to write the perfect first draft. Have them do "Braindancing and Downhilling" (Activity 3) before they try the other activities in this chapter.

Activity 1:
Early Morning Freewrite

> ⤳If you are to have the full benefit of the richness of the unconscious, you must learn to write easily and smoothly when the unconscious is in the ascendant.
>
> —Dorothea Brande

In her wonderful book *Becoming a Writer*, Dorothea Brande points out that the easiest way to release the artist is to write first thing in the morning. Students will see noticeable improvements in their writing if they use this technique regularly, but you must persuade them to do so. Asking "How did the freewrites go this morning?" is a pleasant way to begin a class discussion about writing problems.

Instructions to Students

Put your personal journal and a free-flowing pen on your nightstand before you go to bed. Set your alarm a few minutes earlier than usual. When you wake up the next morning, sit up in bed and begin writing before doing anything else, including brushing your teeth. For a few minutes, write about anything that comes to mind. Don't read your writing; just close your journal and return it to your nightstand.

After you have done this every day for a couple of weeks, we will have a conference to talk about some of the surprising things you'll find in your journal, but don't look at it until then. We'll give you a hint what you'll find when you do look: a lot of junk, yes, but also some writing so terrific you won't believe that you wrote it. We don't know why this happens. Somehow, early in the morning, your artist is awake, even though the rest of you is asleep. It's magic. After a while, you will notice something else: All the other writing you do will seem easier and turn out better—more magic.

Activity 2:
Creative Concentration

> ～What a release to write so that one forgets
> oneself, forgets one's companion, forgets
> where one is or what one is going to do
> next—to be drenched in sleep or in the sea.
> Pencils and pads and curling blue sheets
> alive with letters heap up on the desk.
>
> —Anne Morrow Lindbergh

Many people say that writing takes tough discipline. This is only partly true. What writing absolutely requires is focused concentration. Achieving that concentration requires discipline.

Because a writer who cannot concentrate is in hopeless shape, this activity has become a ritual in our classroom. We use it every drafting day, and on many other days as well. It unfrazzles the frazzled. It retrieves the energies of those who have just returned from P.E. It gives students a sense of being in a special group, and teaches them how to concentrate when they write on their own.

Instructions to Students

The reason concentration is so important is because the artist comes out when you concentrate. Yet concentration is hard to force. Concentrate! you tell yourself while clenching your fists. Sometimes it works. Often, it doesn't. There is another way to concentrate—the artist's way. We call it creative concentration. Have you ever become so involved in doing something you enjoy that you didn't notice the time or what was happening around you? That's creative concentration. It's a little like daydreaming, except that you aren't just dreaming. You are *doing*. Creative concentration is the best kind of concentration for writing.

The steps to creative concentration are quite simple, and they are almost the opposite of clenching your fists and trying to force it:

1. Relax and clear your mind.

2. Focus on what you want to write about.

3. Begin writing and keep going without stopping until you are rolling.

Let's try creative concentration together, as we explain each step:

Step 1: Relax and clear your mind.

For most people, the best time to write is usually early in the morning because they are relaxed and don't have much on their minds. At other times, though, it helps to know how to deliberately relax and clear your mind. There are many ways to do this. Let's try something easy that works for most people:

a. Relax your muscles. You can't clear your mind if your body is tense or wiggling around. Take a good stretch, like a cat (cats are experts at stretching). Stretch all your muscles. Raise your shoulders and try to touch them to the bottoms of your ears, then let your shoulders drop. Stretch your arms as far away from the sides of your body as you can, then rotate your shoulders to make big circles with your hands. Clasp your hands behind your back and bend forward, stretching your arms above your body.

b. Sit down and close your eyes. Beginning with your feet and moving up your body to the top of your head, tense your muscles as tightly as you can. Tense them a little tighter, then suddenly relax.

c. Take deep breaths. With your arms and legs uncrossed and your eyes closed, take a deep breath. Slowly breathe out. Take another deep breath and slowly exhale. Taking a few deep breaths—taking oxygen into your system—is your body's natural way of relaxing.

d. Clear your mind of thoughts. Sit still with your eyes closed and imagine a wall painted all one color. If a thought drifts into your mind, gently push it aside and imagine the wall. Soon, you will be able to imagine the wall without having many other thoughts. You want your mind to be still before doing the next step.

Step 2: Focus on what you want to write about.

Think about the characters, an interesting fact, the first sentence, or anything else about the piece you want to write. Let the thoughts float into your mind. Don't try to organize them. After a couple of minutes, think about what you might write down first. Soon, you'll be ready to begin writing.

Step 3: Begin writing and keep going without stopping until you are rolling.

Now that your concentration is focused, write for five minutes without stopping. If you can't think of anything to write, write "I can't think of anything to write." You don't need to write fast, but keep moving forward. Don't back up to make changes or corrections. The point is to start gently and then keep writing without stopping. It won't be long before you are rolling. It's like starting an old car by rolling it down a hill—that first five minutes is your push to get your "writing car" rolling. If you like braindancing (see Activity 3), braindance for at least five minutes without stopping, then downhill for five minutes.

Activity 3:
Braindancing and Downhilling

∿ True ease in writing comes from art, not chance
As those move easiest who have learned to dance.
—Alexander Pope

This method of persuading the words to flow has many names: Gabriele Rico calls it clustering and webbing in her book *Writing the Natural Way*, which explores using a similar method with many kinds of writing. We once called it brainstorming and fastwriting, but students would choose Wagnerian-sized themes and write like sprinters heading for the tape. The process is much lazier: Let ideas dance to mind, record them quickly, and then slip gracefully down the page like an expert downhill skier, braindancing and downhilling.

"Braindancing and Downhilling," a student favorite, works best with poems, short pieces, or short sections of longer works. It is especially helpful for those who find the physical mechanics of expressing a thought in a sentence so slow that they lose the thought before they finish the sentence. Students enjoy using colored pens and pencils to braindance. Some people have a strong urge to make their writing look pretty; in a first draft, however, they should not. Using pretty colors to braindance satisfies this urge, relieving the pressure they feel to draft beautifully (and perfectly) the first time.

Instructions to Students

Writing is thinking on paper. Have you ever forgotten what you wanted to write while you were writing it? The longer the piece you are writing, the more likely you will bump into this problem. Everybody does, because thinking is fast, but writing is slow. Learning to hold a thought in your mind until you get it on paper takes practice. Braindancing helps you remember your thoughts; downhilling helps you get them down on paper. Recording thoughts in a braindance takes two minutes. Writing them out in sentences—downhilling—takes ten minutes. Braindancing helps you save your thoughts so that you don't forget them.

There's another reason braindancing and downhilling make writing easier: People often think of the end of a story before they think of the beginning. When you braindance, you can record your thoughts in the order they come to you. When you downhill, you can write about them in any order you choose.

Before you begin, get organized:

1. Have several pens and pencils and several sheets of lined notebook paper handy. You don't want to break your concentration by hunting for pens or paper after you've begun.

2. Using a ruler or a straightedge, draw a line down several of the pages you will use for downhilling about three inches from the right-hand side of each page. This is your margin. It should be wide so that you have plenty of room for additions later. Lightly draw a big *X* on the back. It will be easier to edit your writing if you leave margin space. When you downhill, write on every other line. Writing on just one side of the page will allow you to use cut-and-paste editing. Now, get out a couple of clean sheets of paper to use for braindancing.

3. Pick a starting point or writing idea. You can also choose an idea for a section or a scene of a longer piece.

<u>How to Braindance</u>

The braindancing process involves the following steps:

Step 1: Record your writing idea.

On one of the clean sheets of paper, write a word or a phrase in capital letters at the center of the page to represent your starting point or writing idea. If you are working on a section of a longer piece, it represents your idea for that section. Draw a circle around the word or phrase. If you can't think of an idea, use the word *breakfast*—almost everyone can think of something to write about breakfast.

Step 2: Develop creative concentration (see Activity 2).

Step 3: Record your thoughts as they come to you.

To record a thought, write down a couple of words that will help you remember the thought later. For example, suppose you are writing a story about a dog, and one of your thoughts is "This dog chews pink tennis shoes." You can record it by writing "dog shoes" or "pink shoes." The words will remind you of the complete thought.

Draw a circle around each thought after you record it. The circles are important: They separate one thought from another and help you remember each thought. Draw lines to connect thoughts that you think are related. When you have finished, the paper will look like a spiderweb of your thoughts.

Don't try too hard and don't hurry. Also, don't try to decide whether or not the thoughts are good; let the thoughts come and record them, whatever they are. Record thoughts that you may not use in your writing, as well as those you are certain you will use. You won't use all your braindancing thoughts, but if you don't record them all, you might block the flow of ideas. Try to fill the entire page with thoughts.

EXAMPLE

(Note to Teachers: A quick way to demonstrate braindancing is to have students call out ideas as you record them on the blackboard or an overhead transparency.)

Writing Idea: A Story About a Stubborn Dog Named Harry.

(Braindancing thoughts written out in sentences.)

Harry was a mutt that Mom brought home one day. Harry soon tried to rule the entire house. He was picky, too. He insisted on having his own room. He took a pink tennis shoe from my sister's closet and wouldn't give it back. It was his toy, his prize. Finally, when Harry decided to sleep on Dad's bed, Dad got fed up and tried to boot him off. The next morning, Harry was gone, and so was his pink shoe.

How to Downhill

Pick one thought from your braindance and begin writing. Don't hurry; write like an expert skier gliding gently down the slope. Keep writing until you finish your piece. If you are writing a long piece, write a section or a scene in one downhill swoop.

It's important to keep writing. Don't erase or cross out or back up. Fiddling with details and backing up is as bad as skiing uphill. Besides taking a lot of energy, it doesn't work. Fix details and problems later. You want to feel free and easy when you downhill.

Further Tips on
Braindancing and Downhilling

The following points will help you use these techniques:

* If you constantly slow down because you can't remember a word or a spelling or punctuation rule, don't skip over it. Make your best guess, mark it with an "unsure code," and then move on. Unsure codes help you find problems later, so you can fix them when you edit. Print the unsure codes in capital letters inside parentheses, so that later on you can find them easily. You can create your own codes or use the following:

    (SP) = Check spelling.

    (PUNCT) = Check punctuation.

    (WORD) = Find a better word.

    (FACT) = Check this fact.

    (CHECK _____) = Check whatever is noted in the blank space.

* What do you do when you are downhilling and a thought on a different subject comes floating in? You have two options. You can stop downhilling, turn over the page and downhill on that subject for awhile, then return to your original downhill. If you don't want to stop your present downhill, add a word or two to your braindance that will remind you of the thought. Then you can downhill about it later on.

* When you are drafting, you may sometimes bump into what Henriette Klauser calls "the Wall" in *Writing on Both Sides of the Brain*. This is a place where you get stuck—a place writers know well. Here's the trick: Never stop writing at the Wall. Plod along one sentence at a time. Tell yourself that you will keep writing for five more minutes. The Wall can't stop you forever. If you keep plodding along, you will eventually jump the Wall and get rolling again.

◆ Whenever the words won't flow, return to your braindance and add to it until you feel like writing again. If you must stop because you've run out of time, save your braindance for the next time you write. You might also try recopying the last paragraph of your downhill before continuing. Some writers like to edit their previous drafts as a way to begin writing. You can try this, but most beginners find it easier to save editing until they have everything on paper.

Activity 4:
Finding a Writing Place

∽ The place isn't important. The color of ink or typewriter ribbon isn't important. The fancy files behind your desk or table aren't important. Not being distracted from turning out a page or more a day is important.

—Robert Aldeman

Writing takes a tremendous amount of concentration. Most writers aid concentration by choosing a particular place and time to write daily. They can be fanatic about it, especially those who write books. Stories abound of writers who could not finish a book because their favorite restaurant closed or because they remodeled their office and couldn't concentrate in the new one. Many writers are also suspicious of stopping, even for a weekend. Many say they grow cold if they don't write at least every other day.

Students are not writing books, of course, but daily practice in a specified place at a specified time makes a world of difference to their writing. Writing is like playing the piano or golf: The only way to learn to do it is to practice, practice, practice.

Instructions to Students

You won't always have time in school to do all your writing, so your homework assignment is to find at least one good place to write outside school. Professional writers notice which places are best for writing. Once they find a good place, they try to go there to write every day at the same time. They do this to help their concentration. Having a good writing place will make writing easier. There is no particular place that works for everybody, but there are a few basic rules for choosing and using a writing place. Some of you may find that place at home and some of you won't.

Rule 1: Find a place with no distractions.

Talking and writing don't mix. If the words come out of your mouth, they won't flow from your pen. Avoid places where people interrupt you. Avoid places where others talk near you. Avoid places where you will want to talk. Even pieces of paper or books on your desk can be distracting. Avoid messy places, cramped places, and places where you can't move distracting things out of your field of vision. Find a place that doesn't have too many things around to distract you.

Some people find too much *quiet* distracting. They like a little background noise. The trick is to make that noise boring. Foot-tapping music and interesting television programs will distract you. Very soft, slow music might be fine. You might buy cassettes and records of the sounds of nature: birds, waterfalls, raindrops, and so on. These sounds work very well as nondistracting background noise. Very dull television or radio programs work, too.

Rule 2: Write at the same time, in the same place.

Always go to your writing place when you want to write or do research. Try to find a place you can use at the same time every day. Also, avoid doing other things there. It's your writing place—save it for writing.

Rule 3: Keep your materials together.

It's best to store your materials at your writing place. If not, you will need to remember to take your "Starting Points and Writing Ideas Notebook," practice journal, pens, pencils, paper, previous drafts, and other materials with you when you go to your writing place. If you can't keep your materials at your writing place, find a place where you can keep them together.

Rule 4: Notice what helps and what doesn't.

As you use your writing place, notice what helps you and what distracts you. Experiment to make your writing place better. Keep notes on any ideas you have to make your writing place better. Also, make a habit of getting organized before you begin writing. You want to concentrate on writing, not on finding things.

Make a list of places near home or school where you could go to write. Don't forget the library as an option. Make a list of times when you could write at these places. Tonight, show the rules to your parents and ask them to help you find such a place. Tomorrow, show your list to another teacher and ask for suggestions. Bring your list to class tomorrow. We'll discuss the place and time you have chosen and work out any problems you might have.

PART 2:
DIRECTING THE ARTIST

Students should know how to use braindancing and downhilling (see Activity 3) and also must have some confidence with just letting the words flow on paper to get the most out of the activities in this part. These are not one-time activities but favorites we use regularly to inspire and stimulate the drafting process.

Activity 5:
Zoom Lens

> ∽ The oldest books are still only just out to those who have not read them.
>
> —Samuel Butler

Just as six-year-olds have a natural ability to write delightful poetry and eighteen-year-olds have a natural ability to write passionate opinions, twelve- to fifteen-year-olds have a natural ability to write fiction. Their desire to get to the heart of the action, their keen observation of detail, and their strong emotions are all advantages in writing fiction. Teachers are always a little surprised by this observation because so much of the writing they see from students is flat and clichéd. In part, this is natural. A cliché is a good metaphor that has been overused, but it is still new to young people, it is as fresh and funny for them as the day it was coined. Nevertheless, they need to work on using fewer clichés in their writing.

Some teachers try to help students by requiring them to use more adjectives and adverbs. We've tried this ourselves, but it usually produces rather strange pieces littered with words a good editor would cut. We now use the activity "Zoom Lens," which helps students avoid clichés by encouraging their natural talent for detailed observation.

Instructions to Students

Today we are going to practice "Zoom Lens." This writing exercise is based on a favorite old rule of writers: "Show; don't tell." The zoom lens makes drafting easier, and it makes your stories more fun to read because it helps you find interesting details so that you can *show* your reader the characters or settings instead of *telling* your reader about them.

Suppose you are describing a character named Mr. Brown. You could write, "Mr. Brown was nice," but this is not very interesting. It doesn't show us anything about Mr. Brown. "Mr. Brown was wonderfully nice" or "Mr. Brown was charming" are not much better. Readers like details. You want to *show* your reader what your characters are like, don't *tell* your readers about them. In other words, *show* Mr. Brown doing nice things; don't just *tell* your reader he was nice.

EXAMPLE

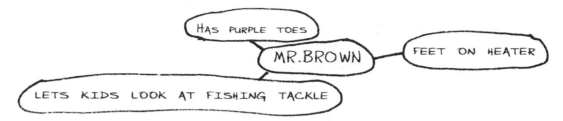

> Mr. Brown had purple toes. He ran a small hardware store in town, the kind of store that had one of just about everything. Sunday afternoons, when business was slow, he'd sit up front and let me wander through the store. My favorite section was the fishing tackle. I'd gloat over every new spinner and weight, dreaming that some day I could actually buy one. He'd take off his shoes and socks and put his feet right on top of the small electric heater he kept by the cash register. I asked him once why his feet didn't burn.
>
> "See them toes?" he said. "They're purple. Cold as ice all winter. Can't get 'em warmed up enough to burn."

See how much more interesting Mr. Brown is when the writer shows Mr. Brown being nice? In the course of describing Mr. Brown, the writer also reveals a lot about the story: The reader learns that it takes place in a small town, and also learns that the narrator—the character who is telling the story—is a kid who likes to look at fishing tackle.

How to Play Zoom Lens

Step 1: Create a picture of a character in your mind. Imagine your character in a specific place—the setting.

Step 2: Pretend to be a camera operator filming the scene. Look at your scene through the camera.

Step 3: Once you have the scene set in your mind, zoom in on at least three details about what your character looks like, what your character is doing, or how your character is feeling.

Step 4: Use the details from step 3 to write a paragraph or two describing the character or the setting, or both.

In your practice journal, use the zoom lens to describe a character.

The zoom lens helps you describe settings. Usually, you don't describe the setting all at once. You describe it bit by bit as the action of the story takes place. Suppose you want to describe part of the setting by describing a character looking at the sunset. You could write, "The sky was beautiful," or you could use the zoom lens to show your reader details.

EXAMPLE

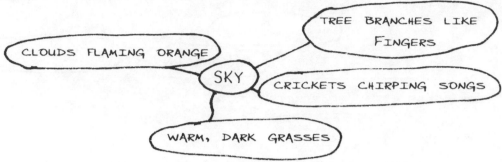

> Joe stared at the setting sun, watching the clouds flame orange
> and melt soft pink. The trees stood in a row along the crest of the hill,
> the black-fingered branches dancing with a gentle joy to the songs of
> crickets in the warm, dark grass.
> "I can never leave this place," he sighed.

See how much better a reader can imagine the sunset when the writer shows flame-colored clouds and tree branches like fingers?

In your practice journal, try using the zoom lens to describe a setting.

If you are having a hard time imagining a scene, try using the zoom lens to find at least three details for each of the five senses. Begin with something simple, such as "girl sitting on a rock." Pretend you're the girl. Make up at least three details describing how it smells, tastes, feels, sounds, and looks to be sitting on that rock. Finally, describe how the girl is feeling at that moment. You probably won't use all the details you create, but it's better to have too many details to choose from than too few.

EXAMPLE

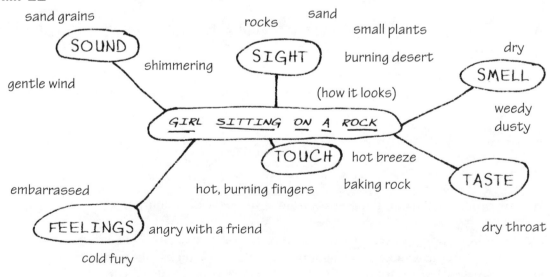

> Mary crouched down and tested the warmth of the rock with her
> fingertips before settling herself upon it. She stared across miles of
> shimmering rock and sand. Usually, the dusty smell and the gentle
> press of the hot breeze calmed her. But not today. Today, the desert
> brought with it cold fury.

When you have dull "tell" writing, it is usually trying to report something that a character experienced with one of the five or six human senses: sound, sight, smell, touch, taste (and emotion). For example, "Carol heard the bell." "Show" writing tries to pull the reader right in by showing the reader what the character is seeing, feeling, hearing, and so forth; for example, "The bell boomed through Carol's ears. On and on it rang until she thought the noise would drive her mad."

In your practice journal, try using the zoom lens with the five senses to write a description of either a character or a setting.

Have you ever said, "I'm bored"? Well, the zoom lens is just the technique for you. You can use it to help you describe a character's mood, with words such as *bored*, *happy*, or *frightened*. For example, imagine yourself in a place that is boring. Use the zoom lens to find at least three details of the scene (use the five senses, if you need more details). Then write a couple of paragraphs of a story about a character who is bored, without using the words *bored* or *boring*.

If you find yourself using any of the words in the following list, this is a good clue that it's time to try the zoom lens. They tend to pop up next to the word *was* (or *is*) when you are telling, not showing.

TELL WORDS

About Characters	About Settings
was a pain in the neck	was beautiful
was bored	was boring
was dumb	was cold
was friendly	was dark
was funny	was dirty
was interesting	was empty
was lazy	was scary
was nice	was spooky
was pretty (or beautiful)	was strange
was sad	was sunny
was smart	was warm
was tall, dark, and handsome	was weird
was terrific	was wet
was ugly	was wild
was weird	was yucky

Additional Notes to Teachers

♦ Add dull adjectives and clichés from students' writing to the list of tell words.

Activity 6:
Hooks and Leaders

~ Beginning a book is unpleasant . . . Worse than
not knowing your subject is not knowing how
to treat it, because that's finally everything.

—Phillip Roth

Many students can't get started because they have so much trouble writing the first sentence. This activity provides them with some first-sentence models to help them over the hump.

Instructions to Students

The opening of your piece is worth special consideration. You want it to grab your readers' attention and then tempt them to keep reading. It helps to think of your opening as two sentences: the hook, to grab your readers' attention, and the leader, to tempt them to keep reading. Hooks and leaders can be longer than one sentence, of course, but be careful not to lose your reader.

Writing an opening is like fishing: The fish bites your hook, then you pull the fish into the boat with your leader. What hooks a reader? Information, surprise, or suspense. What leads the reader into the piece? Knowing a little bit about what is to come, but not everything. In fiction, the leader sets up a little puzzle to be solved by reading further. In nonfiction, the leader promises more information to the reader who keeps reading.

You can write your hook and leader at any time. Some writers use anything that comes to mind for a first sentence, just to get started. Then they rewrite the opening after they finish the piece. Others like to write a polished opening before they begin drafting the rest. Either way, it helps to try several different openings, then pick the one that you like best.

There are thousands of kinds of hooks and leaders. In the "Hooks and Leaders" handout, we've listed ten different kinds of hooks to give you some ideas. Let's discuss two of them in detail: the shocker and the summary hooks. We need a writing idea to begin. Let's pretend that we want to write a fantasy story about a girl and a dragon. We'll name the girl Jesse. Fantasies often have magicians, many of them named Merlin. We like magicians, so we'll make up one—Marlon the Magician. (We are quite sure you can invent more creative names, but these names will do for now.)

First, we'll write a shocker hook. The shocker hook surprises the reader and creates suspense. The hook presents an attention-catching, life-or-death (or at least dangerous) situation, and then the leader creates a little suspense.

(In the following examples, the hook is italic; the rest of the opening is the leader.)

EXAMPLE

Fiction Shocker Hook

A purple dragon can change your life or squash you flat. When Marlon sent the dragon to Jesse, he couldn't be sure which would happen. He just hoped for the best.

Not bad. The shocker hook presents a scary possibility: getting squashed by a dragon. The leader presents a puzzle. We learn that Marlon sent the dragon, but we don't know everything. If dragons are so dangerous, why did he send it? Does he hate Jesse? No. The next sentence says that Marlon hoped for the best. He's worried. Perhaps he was forced to send the dragon, but we don't know why or what will happen unless we keep reading.

The summary hook grabs the reader with interesting, but incomplete information. It provides bits and pieces of who, what, when, where, why, and how in one sentence with an implied invitation to read on to find out more. Again, we'll use a leader that creates a little mystery or suspense.

EXAMPLE

Fiction Summary Hook

(who)   (what)   (where)

When Jesse saw the purple dragon appear in the meadow

(when)   (why)

on Friday she knew Marlon the Magician sent it. Marlon always

sent something on Friday and it usually caused trouble.

In this example, the leader creates several little mysteries. What is the relationship between Marlon and Jesse? Why should he send things to her? Why on Friday? Is this dragon going to cause trouble? What kind? We must keep reading to solve these mysteries!

Hooks and leaders help with nonfiction openings, too. We need an idea to begin. Let's use "why people should buckle their seatbelts" and try shocker and summary hooks and leaders.

EXAMPLE

Nonfiction Shocker Hook

Don't buckle up this morning, and you could be dead by noon.

If people knew the facts they would buckle up more often.

Nonfiction Summary Hook

(who)   (how)   (what)

Each time you buckle your seatbelt, you reduce your chances

(when)

of being killed or injured that day by fifty percent. Why do people

who try to protect themselves in so many other ways so often fail

to buckle up?

The summary hook explains or implies who, what, why, when, where, and how for an interesting fact. The leader promises information about why people don't buckle their seatbelts. Those of you who have worked with prewriting choices (see "Prewriting Choices for Nonfiction, Chapter 2, Activity 1) will notice that the leader in nonfiction openings frequently presents the key idea for the piece.

Practice writing some hooks and leaders. Choose a writing idea and try writing at least three different hooks and leaders for a story or nonfiction piece. Use the "Hooks and Leaders" handout for ideas. When you have finished, choose the hook and leader you think is most effective.

(Text continues on p. 93.)

Hooks and Leaders

<u>Student Handout</u>

There are as many first sentences as there are stories and writers. You might want to collect the first sentences of other writers and study them. Write your own versions. In this handout are ten types of hooks, each followed by a leader (the hook is italic; the rest of the opening is the leader).

You will probably notice that our hooks and leaders get you off to a fast start. Longer pieces and more academic pieces often have more leisurely openings. The ideas here can help you when you are stuck, but if a good first sentence comes to you naturally, use it.

1. **Shocker:** The shocker hook opens the piece with a life-or-death (or at least dangerous) situation.

EXAMPLE

Fiction

A purple dragon can change your life or squash you flat. When Marlon sent the dragon to find Jesse, he couldn't be sure which would happen. He just hoped for the best.

Nonfiction

If you don't buckle up this morning, you could be dead by noon. If people knew the facts, they would buckle up more often.

2. **Summary:** The summary hook tells the reader a little bit about who, what, when, where, why, and how in one sentence.

EXAMPLE

Fiction

When Jesse saw the purple dragon appear in the meadow one Friday, she knew Marlon the Magician had sent it. Marlon always sent something on Friday, and it usually caused trouble.

Nonfiction

Each time you buckle your seatbelt, you reduce your chances of being killed or injured by fifty percent. Seatbelts have saved more lives in the past twenty years than any other human invention.

3. **Capsule:** The capsule hook opens the piece with a brief summary.

EXAMPLE

Fiction

Marlon the Magician sent something every Friday, and it usually caused trouble. The purple dragon was no exception. Jesse, of course, didn't know that this particular purple dragon had been sent to save her life.

Nonfiction

Seatbelts have saved more lives in the past twenty years than any other human invention. Even more lives can be saved if we take a few seconds to buckle up each time we get in a car.

4. **Definition:** The definition hook begins with a definition, either from a dictionary or one you write.

EXAMPLE

Fiction

Dragons are huge, terrifying beasts with beautiful, jeweled eyes and disgusting breath. The friendly ones are purple. It was one of the purple variety that met Jesse in a meadow one Friday.

Nonfiction

A seatbelt is something you spend three seconds buckling to save three years in the hospital. The simple act of buckling up each time you get in a car reduces your chances of being injured or killed by fifty percent.

5. **Problem:** The problem hook briefly suggests a problem that you will solve in the piece.

EXAMPLE

Fiction

If a large purple dragon drops into a meadow in front of you one day, it won't go away until you understand why it came. Jesse knew Marlon had sent the dragon, but she hadn't the faintest idea why.

Nonfiction

Most people's biggest problem when driving is getting their passengers to buckle up. The best way to accomplish this life-saving task is to explain the facts.

6. **Question:** The question hook asks a question that you will answer in the piece.

EXAMPLE

Fiction

The question for Jesse was this: What do you do with a large, purple dragon? Hers landed in front of her in a meadow one Friday afternoon. Obviously, Marlon had sent it, but she had no idea why.

Nonfiction

Before you start your car, do you check to be certain all your passengers are buckled up? You can save money, time, and grief with a two-second check.

7. **Statement of Authority:** The statement of authority hook is most often used by experts writing about their subject of expertise. You can use it, too, provided you show why you or one of your characters is an expert.

EXAMPLE

Fiction

When Marlon sends you a purple dragon, he has a good reason. I know. He sent me one, and it caused no end of trouble. (In this case the expert is Jesse.)

Nonfiction

According to a survey I took of students in my school, only thirty percent of them buckle their seatbelts every time they get into a car. They might buckle up more often if they knew the facts. (You are the expert because you did the survey.)

8. **Quotation:** The quotation hook begins with a quote, from a person or from a book, magazine, or newspaper, that fits the story or subject. For fiction, you can make up people, books, magazines, and newspapers to quote.

EXAMPLE

Fiction

"In 3050 King Fardmen declared the last dragon dead."—The History of the House of Fardmen. Jesse had read the famous history of her country written by the scholar Quiliman, and she knew it was wrong, particularly on the subject of dragons. One Friday, more than 150 years after the King had declared dragons extinct, a large, purple dragon appeared before her. Dead? No. This dragon was most certainly alive, at least lively enough to cause her no end of trouble.

Nonfiction

"I know I should wear seatbelts, but I often don't," said Bill Bramer, a student at Leschi Middle School. According to my survey, Bill is like many students at Leschi. More than seventy percent of those surveyed said that often they did not buckle their seatbelts.

9. **Statistics:** The statistics hook cites a statistic that leads into the piece. For fiction, you can make up a source.

EXAMPLE

Fiction

According to the Fardmen Daily Screamer, *more than eighty percent of all dragon sightings in the year 4101 were somehow connected to one man, the Magician named Marlon.* Experts claimed that this statistic was pure twaddle. They maintained that both the Magician Marlon and dragons were myths. Jesse never believed in the magician, but the day a large, purple dragon appeared before her, she knew Marlon had sent it.

Nonfiction

One in every eight people will be involved in an automobile accident at least once in their lives. Even a minor fender-bender can produce serious injuries if the passengers are not wearing seatbelts.

10. **Comparison or Contrast:** The comparison or contrast hook compares two things for similarities, contrasts them for differences, or both.

EXAMPLE

Fiction

(contrasting girls to dragons) *Young, headstrong girls and dragons have little in common. Girls can rarely be successfully ordered around, whereas dragons are always under orders, usually those of a magician. Girls laugh at magicians; dragons worship them. Girls are sometimes pretty; dragons are always gorgeous, if you can ignore their stink.* Getting a girl together with a dragon is difficult, but this was the Magician Marlon's task one Friday when he sent a large, purple dragon to meet a girl named Jesse.

Nonfiction

(contrasting what can happen in thirty seconds) It takes thirty seconds to buckle the average seatbelt and the same amount of time to die without one. People who do not use seatbelts are twice as likely to die in an accident as those who do.

From *Teaching Writing in Middle School.* © 1998 Beth Means and Lindy Lindner. Teacher Ideas Press. (800) 237-6124.

Activity 7:
Warm-Ups for Cold Days

～You don't start with any aesthetic manifesto,
you just do what works.

—E. L. Doctorow

Writing can wax hot and cold. Students, like all writers, may have trouble getting started because they are writing cold that day. In the "Warm-Ups" handout, we've collected ideas to help students get started on those cold days. Students enjoy doing these activities in their practice journals, independent of any writing assignment.

Instructions to Students

When you begin writing regularly (every day or every other day), you will begin to notice something strange about writing. Some days, writing is very easy—you are writing hot and nothing can stop you. Other days are just the opposite—you are writing cold and it is hard to get started. There is nothing wrong with you; this is the way of writing.

You should not stop writing just because you are having a cold day. What you need to do is get warmed up. We have a handout listing some ideas for warming up on cold days. Save it; it's a handy list.

(Text continues on p. 97.)

Warm-Ups

<u>Student Handout</u>

Concentrate on following your writing routine. Don't worry about the deadline or the entire piece; just worry about the part of your piece that you want to write today.

- Try to write poorly. Natalie Goldberg, in her book *Writing Down the Bones*, calls this *"composting."* Gardeners compost old leaves and vegetable matter as the basis of their garden soil. You are preparing to write the piece later by writing garbage now. Let it compost in the back of your mind for awhile. Eventually a flower of a story or poem might grow from the compost.

- Tell yourself that you will keep working for five minutes more. Then, if it still isn't going well, you can try something else.

- Work on two pieces at once. If you are writing cold on one, switch to the other.

- Pick another section of the piece and begin there. If you are stuck on the beginning, write the ending or the climax.

- Change your tools: Switch to a different pen. Write on a tiny pad of paper. Write on a big art pad using big, bright pens. If you are using a computer, switch off the monitor. Tell your story to a tape recorder—or to yourself.

- Draw a picture of your story, then write about it.

- Edit and recopy a section you have already drafted.

- Try "Braindancing and Downhilling" (Activity 3), "Zoom Lens" (Activity 5), "Hooks and Leaders" (Activity 6), or "Follow the Leader" (Activity 8).

- Hold a conference with your teacher or a member of your writing group. Explain why you are having trouble and ask for suggestions.

- Pretend that you are someone else writing about the same subject. For example, if you are writing about a porcupine, pretend to be the porcupine. If you are writing a romance, pretend to be a Martian anthropologist visiting Earth, and write a letter home explaining the romance.

- Write about whatever is in front of you. Close your eyes, turn your head, and open your eyes. Describe whatever you see, in detail. Then describe the things around it. Once you have warmed up, begin writing a scene for your piece using that description. For example, suppose you have described a crack in the linoleum. Write a scene for your piece in which one of your characters is looking at a crack in the linoleum.

- Try writing your piece in a different genre. Write your essay as a song, your story as a how-to, your film script as a poem, your news article as a short story, or your personal experience as a letter.

- Braindance backwards (see Activity 3): Draw a pretty web of circles and lines, then fill in the circles with whatever ideas seem appropriate.

◆ Forget that you are writing about something in particular, just begin writing and keep writing. Don't even try to write sentences. Write single words, or thoughts or feelings. Write anything at all.

◆ Write backwards. Write the last sentence of a paragraph, then the sentence preceding it, then the sentence preceding that, working back to the first sentence.

◆ Borrow a few words to begin a first sentence.

EXAMPLES

I remember . . .

You wouldn't think that . . .

I have never . . .

For the past two years, I . . .

The last time I . . .

If you have never . . .

You think you know how to _____ until you . . .

A good friend can . . .

This morning was the first time I . . .

If you are writing fiction, you may prefer to change these starter sentences to the third person, past tense.

EXAMPLES

He (she) remembered . . .

He (she) never thought that . . .

He (she) had never . . .

Make a connection between your subject and something unrelated and write about that. For example, suppose you are writing about the American Revolution. Look around. How are the things you see connected to the American Revolution? For example, how are your tennis shoes connected to the American Revolution? Use your connection as a first sentence of a warm-up paragraph. Go ahead! Be ridiculous!

EXAMPLES

How are tennis shoes connected to the American Revolution?

The tennis shoe was invented to help George Washington sneak up on the British.

How are fluorescent lights connected to the American Revolution?

Ben Franklin snapped on the fluorescent light and then . . .

◆ Make up a starter sentence. Fold a piece of paper in half lengthwise. On the first half (so that when you unfold the paper this half will be on the left), make a list of subjects—human, animal, vegetable, mineral, or any other category. On the other half, make a list of unusual verbs. Use a thesaurus or a dictionary for help (you may choose verbs you don't know, but look up the definitions). Unfold the paper and write a sentence using each subject-verb pair. Then write about anything the sentences suggest.

EXAMPLE

handwriting	grumble
anteaters	joust
loneliness	poise

My handwriting grumbles onto the page.

Each night, anteaters joust with a thousand prey.

Loneliness is poised on my doorstep.

**Activity 8:
Follow the Leader**

> The instruction we find in books is like fire. We fetch it from our neighbors, kindle it at home, communicate it to others, and it becomes the property of all.
>
> —Voltaire

It's a paradox that much about writing cannot be explained in words, any more than words alone can explain a piece of music. "Follow the Leader" is the writer's version of listening and humming along to music. For students who have not yet read widely, listening to writing is vital if they are to develop a strong sense of what they are trying to accomplish. Playing "Follow the Leader" is simple: Choose a scene, section, paragraph, or sentence of a published work. Discuss it briefly, read it aloud, and ask students to write their version, following the writer's lead.

We use "Follow the Leader" whenever we explain a new writing term or whenever we want students to try a particular technique (see "Teacher's Notebook: On Writing Terms," Chapter 2; see Chapter 4 for nonfiction techniques and Chapter 5 for fiction techniques). If we want students to develop good characterization, we read a few paragraphs with good characterization; if we want students to develop dialogue, we begin by reading dialogue. If we want to teach a rule of punctuation, we read an appropriate sentence aloud, including all the correct punctuation marks, while students write it on paper. Then we ask them to write their own sentences following that example. "Follow the Leader" is a wonderful way to get students started, and it is a simple method for clarifying what you want students to try without getting tangled up in windy explanations.

Instructions to Students

Reading and writing go together. The more you read, the easier it is to write; the more you write, the more interested you are in reading. One way to learn about writing is to play "Follow the Leader." Choose a few paragraphs from a story or an article that you like. Read the text aloud and then braindance and downhill (see Activity 3) to write your version. Let's try it with a scene from James Herriot's *All Creatures Great and Small* (Bantam, 1978, p. 12). Herriot is one of our favorite authors for "Follow the Leader." His beautifully described scenes about everyday life will inspire you to write with depth and imagination. For those of you who haven't read his books, Herriot is a country veterinarian in the north of England.

In this scene, he is coming to the door of a clinic to interview for a job, and he meets Mrs. Hall, the housekeeper. As you read the scene, notice a couple of things: Not much happens in the scene. Herriot rings the doorbell and Mrs. Hall answers it. That's the entire plot. Also, notice the details—how Herriot describes the door and the dogs. It's the little details that make scenes interesting, not necessarily what happens.

When you have finished reading the scene, get out your practice journals. Make up a character and give the character a name, and make up a house. Write a brief scene about what happens to your character at the house. Your version doesn't need to be like Herriot's—it's your story—except that you should try to use as much detail as Herriot uses when you tell your story.

EXAMPLES

(These unedited examples come from a sixth-, seventh-, and eighth-grade writing workshop just as they were turned in. Spelling, grammar, punctuation, and paragraphing have not been edited.)

When we got to the porch, I rang the doorbell. Nobody answered. I turned the door handle and opened the door. We walked in to take a look around. We looked everywhere in the house. There was only one place left, the basement. When we got down to the basement, we saw a crazy looking man, his hair was sticking up, he had a big long nose with a pimple in each nostril, and his clothes were made of trash he found in a garbage can. My friend elbowed me and whispered to me, "He looks like something you'd find in the toilet." He stared at me and then at my friend, then he said he was expecting us. He told us he was a scientist, and he wanted us to test some sort of machine for him. My friend said, "Forget you!" and we both started to run upstairs to escape, but the door shut automatically. We were trapped.

—A seventh-grader

As I was turning, I could see on each side of me emerald green grass, perfectly cut. On the outside of the grass, I could see many beautiful purple and red flowers all standing in a row. When I reached the step, an old cat was lying there, purring softly. When I reached the door, I could see the perfectly cut wood that was carved into the door. As I rang the doorbell, a sound of soothing music floated towards me. When the door finally opened, a beautiful, but older lady came and opened the door. She was the best looking lady I had ever seen. She wore a blue shawl with dark blue pants. Her face was absolutely perfect. She had blue eyes and grayish-white hair. Her nose and mouth were just perfect.

Her house was all white and very clean. She asked me what I wanted. I told her I was collecting paper delivery money.

—A sixth-grader

"Hey! Where is everyone?" I screeched at the top of my voice as I burst into the front door. "Oh great," I thought, "my first day here and my parents want to abandon me."

I walked into the living room. It was still empty, but the dining room furniture was already arranged. There were a few boxes lying around, but I was wondering where all the other furniture was.

I had just walked into the kitchen when I heard a car door slam. Then it was followed by a burst of screaming and shouting from outside. "Well, obviously, Dad's home," I sighed.

"Can you believe it! Well, I can't!" he hollered. I was sure the entire neighborhood could hear him.

"What happened?" I asked, hoping he wouldn't have another outburst.

"Would you believe that, because of some mix-up, half of our furniture actually got sent to Egypt! Now some wierdos will be enjoying our furniture while we sleep on the floor tonight!"

Now it was my turn to scream my head off. "Egypt!" I hollered. I stood there in disbelief.

—A seventh-grader

Additional Notes to Teachers

◆ Use good published examples. There is little point in asking students to study and follow the example of poor or unedited writing. You don't necessarily need to find samples written at your students' reading level. They can handle surprisingly sophisticated material when it is read to them, and their writing in turn is often equally sophisticated.

◆ If you are using "Follow the Leader" to explain a writing term or to demonstrate a writing technique, do the activity twice, using the work of two writers. Most students will have trouble applying the term or technique in a general way without having modeled at least two examples.

◆ "Follow the Leader" provides a good opportunity for a discussion of plagiarism. "Follow the Leader" is not plagiarism. Being inspired by another writer is not the same as copying another's work and calling it one's own. The first is a good way to learn; the second is stealing. "Follow the Leader" is an excellent way to show students the difference.

◆ In *Writing a Novel from Plot to Print*, Lawrence Block explains that the best way to learn outlining is to imitate good outlines, that is, to outline other people's work to understand how they put it together. Having students outline their favorite published work is a wonderful exercise.

◆ Try reading a few simple paragraphs aloud while students write them in their practice journals. Read all the punctuation, spell any words the students might misspell, and tell them when to begin a new paragraph. Discuss the section with the group (don't forget to explain that copying for practice is not plagiarism, as long as it stays in the practice journal).

This dictation method is standard practice in the French school system, and French students tend to paragraph beautifully, even though the paragraph is not formally taught. We suspect that routine copying of published paragraphs may be one of the best ways to teach paragraphing.

◆ Good fiction and poetry examples can be found everywhere. We use a rather eclectic collection, carefully selecting samples from genre writers, favorite writers, and a few well above the students' reading level. Here's our book list:

Alice in Wonderland by Lewis Carroll

All Creatures Great and Small and *James Herriot's Dog Stories* by James Herriot

Bridge to Terabithia by Katherine Paterson

Dog Days of Arthur Cane by T. Ernesto Bethancourt

The Dragonriders of Pern by Anne McCaffrey

Fantastic Voyage by Isaac Asimov

A Fine and Pleasant Misery; Never Sniff a Gift Fish; and *They Shoot Canoes, Don't They?* by Patrick F. McManus

The Gammage Cup by Carol Kendall

Gulag Archipelago by Alexsandr I. Solzhenitsyn

Hangin' Out with Cici by Francine Pascal

The Hobbit by J. R. R. Tolkien

How to Eat Like a Child by Delia Ephron

I, Robot by Isaac Asimov

If I Were in Charge of the World & Other Worries by Judith Viorst (poetry)

Just-So Stories by Rudyard Kipling

Lad: A Dog by Albert Payson Terhune

Dogsong and *Mr. Tuckett* by Gary Paulsen

The Racing Game (Odds Against) and *Reflex* by Dick Francis

The Ransom of Red Chief by O. Henry

Rocannon's World by Ursula K. LeGuin

Scary Poems for Rotten Kids by Sean Ohuigin

To Build a Fire by Jack London

The Veldt by Ray Bradbury

Where the Sidewalk Ends: Poems & Drawings by Shel Silverstein

The Wind in the Willows by Kenneth Grahame

Sackett's Land by Louis L'Amour

♦ We like to use nonfiction examples that are close to our students' reading level, but it doesn't hurt them to hear great nonfiction essayists. Well-written formal nonfiction for young students is hard to find; less-formal nonfiction is everywhere. We begin with the newspapers and popular magazines, most of which are written at the eighth- to ninth-grade reading level. Our favorites are *Popular Science*, *Ladies Home Journal*, *Consumer Reports*, *National Geographic*, *Sports Illustrated*, *The Yankee*, *Time for Kids*, *Zoobooks*, and (of course) *The Writer* and *Writer's Digest*. Regional magazines often have interesting stories about local history and travel. Check nearby zoos, aquariums, and museums—many publish a magazine or newsletter with stories about subjects that students can see for themselves (the same applies to local companies and government). We also like to ask students to bring to class samples of nonfiction—everything from the instructions on soup cans to their favorite magazines—for a class treasury of good examples.

To use more difficult or older works, it's best to explain the background and read the entire piece aloud, then excerpt brief, simple segments. Older students can handle essays, particularly the informal essays of E. B. White (*Essays of E. B. White*), S. J. Perelman (*The Best of S. J. Perelman*), and James Thurber (*Thurber's Dogs* or *The Thurber Album*). *The Bedford Reader*, edited by X. J. Kennedy and Dorothy M. Kennedy, is an excellent collection of essays organized by technique (some can be excerpted for ninth- and tenth-grade students).

More and more science writers are writing popular versions of their technical papers, and many are appropriate for students. Our favorite is *The Lives of a Cell: Notes of a Biology Watcher by Lewis Thomas*.

♦ Those magic words "for a transcript, send $2.00" are almost always worth following, particularly if students can see the videotape and compare it to the script.

TEACHER'S NOTEBOOK

On Remembering Writing

By the time we write our last research paper and leave college, we all tend to anchor our writing to shore and never cast out to sea again. It's easy to forget what we ask of students when most of our own writing is telephone messages, grocery lists, and notes to parents.

For many students—especially those still struggling with spelling or the mechanics of holding the pen—writing may seem about as natural as learning to swing a golf club. You may be out of touch with this feeling if you haven't recently held a long club in a miserably uncomfortable grip and tried to swing smoothly as you bend your knees, keep your head still, shift your weight, don't raise your hip, keep your left arm straight, and remember which direction you are hitting the ball. "Relax!" says the coach. It's a wonder that golf coaches aren't clubbed to death. Students have similar thoughts about their writing teachers.

It's much easier to teach students to write if you are grappling with writing something yourself, even if it's only a few early-morning thoughts in a personal journal. Write with your students. It's good for them to see adults writing. Set aside writing time in class and teach students to respect the privacy of those who are trying to write by insisting that they not interrupt you.

If you can't think of anything to write about, look at your class and pick any student. Write a brief scene sketching a moment in the classroom with your student—the setting, what you said, how you felt. Don't pick a big moment; pick a small one, as brief as a glance.

Set aside a Saturday morning to go to the library, a local café, or even the airport for a few hours of uninterrupted drafting. Later, write about what it felt like to draft stories alone. Share your observations with your students.

If you begin writing yourself, you will notice (among other things) that concentrated drafting is exhausting. Three or four hours is about the maximum an adult can handle during a day. In class, you'll always find at least one student who won't have enough energy to write that day. Develop classroom writing jobs, such as organizing the reference books, typing, copyediting, drawing illustrations, making book covers, or taking care of the background cassettes if you play sounds of nature or background music as aids to concentration. Assign these jobs to students who are too tired write.

On Giving Assignments

As we have been saying, the key to getting the words to flow on paper but still having quality is to separate the artist from the craftsman. The artist handles drafting while the craftsman handles the planning and the editing. To keep these two different roles separated, teachers need to be especially careful when giving assignments. The standard assignment mixes them up: "Your assignment is to research (craftsman) and write (the artist for drafting, the craftsman for editing) on the Civil War. It must be at least two pages, spelling and punctuation count (craftsman)." Giving such an assignment predictably results in a spate of hysterical questions about margins and typing versus handwriting, adding to the confusion. It is better to have the students think of a lot of potential ideas for papers and save them in their writing ideas notebook, thereby getting the artist's first task out of the way. Later you can give an assignment selecting one of those ideas to develop further with research and planning—strictly craftsman's work. When that's done, assign the drafting. When the rough draft is done, assign the editing. When editing is done, assign the production (be it recopying neatly or printing out on a word processor), sometimes complete with book covers and illustrations. Breaking up the traditional assignment into these different, discrete tasks, makes the total assignment less daunting and ensures that the artist's role and the craftsman's stay well separated.

On Time in Class for Writing

Always set aside time in class for writing. It's the most important time you spend. Students may not be able to find a good writing environment at home, and they have questions best answered by teachers, not parents. Without answers they bog down. By the next day, they have forgotten the questions. Also, if students never write in school, many privately conclude that writing isn't important.

If there isn't time to do all the planning, drafting, and editing in class, at least set aside a few minutes in class to have students begin the assignment. Gathering that first bit of momentum may be the most difficult part of writing. A running start in class makes it easier to battle through all the distractions at home.

NOTES
FROM THE PROS

On Talking About It

Many books about teaching writing suggest (as we do) that students talk about what they are going to write while they plan, but the professionals tend to share Norman Mailer's view: "It's hard to talk about one's present work, for it spoils something at the root of the creative act. It discharges tension." Some students may feel that talking about their work makes drafting more difficult, though others find talking helpful. The middle course may be best. Encourage students to discuss the possibilities for a piece before they draft. Discuss the piece with them during drafting only if they have a problem. Once they have an idea for a solution, send them back to the desk, saying, "Don't tell me; write it down."

Nonfiction Workshop

MEANS

INTRODUCTION

After about age twelve or so, young students become dissatisfied with their writing if it doesn't sound at least a little like the adult writing they read. If they don't learn some technique at this stage, some decide that they can't write. Most rely on advice from older brothers and sisters to try to make their writing sound more grown-up. Every teacher knows the homegrown "Student Manual of Style":

Big-Word Babble: Use every big word you can remember and make your sentences sound fancy. (Some students forget the sentences and just write all the big words they know. All of them forget to say anything. Big-word babble is all sound and no meaning.)

Give-'em-What-They-Like Syndrome: Just sprinkle in a few words like *however*, *in conclusion*, and *moreover*. Be sure to include *thus* and *therefore* to keep the teacher happy. (The alternate version is to choose a few good vocabulary words from this week's list or the thesaurus and toss them in at random. Again, writing something with meaning is secondary.)

Copy-the-Encyclopedia Syndrome: Just copy it out of the encyclopedia to make it sound good. Change a few words here and there to make it your own. (Many students don't even check to see if the borrowed section makes any sense in context. It sounds good, and that's all they want.)

The antidote to these rules is solid, technical information. Many people don't realize what an enormous fund of technical knowledge even poor adult writers have. The average professional writer may know as many as 500 more specialized writing techniques than the average adult does. We use the term *technique* loosely. A technique can be almost anything: a rule of punctuation, writing tips, a concept (e.g., what's a *scene*), a writing rule, or ideas, such as improving the quality of a description by making it more specific. Every time students ask "How can I . . .?" they want to know a technique. Even sixth-grade students can ask some real stumpers.

Part 1 presents two activities to help students learn to structure a nonfiction paragraph. Part 2, "A Catalog of Nonfiction Techniques," presents an alphabetical listing of techniques—anecdotes, comparison and contrast, conclusions, definitions, division and classification, examples, and transitions—each with an explanation, examples, and "Tricks of the Trade" (tips for using the technique). We use "Follow the Leader" (Chapter 3, Activity 8) to introduce the techniques.

There are thousands of techniques from which to choose. For this chapter, we have chosen those that are most often used in nonfiction and that help students develop the supporting sentences they need to construct paragraphs. Those techniques that seem to satisfy the urge to sound more adult are discussed with fiction (see Chapter 5).

The division between nonfiction and fiction is a bit arbitrary on our part. Although description and narrative are covered with fiction, both are obviously an important technique for nonfiction as well. Comparisons, which we classify as nonfiction, are regularly used in fiction. Don't hesitate to go back and forth between the two chapters; it helps. Fiction helps students develop fluency and a sense of detail that will improve their nonfiction, whereas nonfiction will help them begin to grasp structure, paragraphing, and the effect of prewriting choices—ideal reader, purpose, mood, and key idea (see Chapter 2, Activity 2). Taken together, nonfiction and fiction skills will produce a better writer. It is sometimes more efficient to teach a technique using fiction with students this age. For example, first asking them to describe a person, place, or thing in their story using specific imaginary details; then ask them to describe a real person, place or thing using factual and accurate details. Trying to explain what transitions do is much easier to explain with fiction, where characters physically move to a new place or time, than nonfiction, where the writer is moving from one abstract concept to the next. Once students understand fiction transitions, they will find it easier to grasp that instead of moving from one place or time to another, they are moving from one concept or category to the next. They may still write clumsy transitions, but they will have a better idea of when to make a transition.

Two Approaches
to Teaching Nonfiction

Many teachers struggle with teaching nonfiction in middle school. Though students have a natural ability to write fiction at this age, they have not yet fully developed the skills they need to write nonfiction, such as connecting cause with effect, categorizing, distinguishing specific from general, and so forth. You can take one of two approaches: Saturate them with techniques, give them lots of practice, and wait for them to catch on; or walk them through nonfiction slowly, showing them one technique at a time. We tend to use the first approach most of the time, saving the second approach for those who seem lost and discouraged.

Learning to write is like learning to drive in that one is learning to do several things simultaneously; each thing is a complicated task in itself. For those who are struggling, it helps to relieve them of one or more of the tasks while they learn a new one. You can, for example, write a topic sentence and have students write the supporting sentences, then write the supporting sentences and have students practice writing a topic sentence. When they have tried that a few times, have them rewrite the supporting sentences using particular techniques, such as examples, comparisons, or definitions.

Coping with the Fact Problem

With nonfiction, pay special attention to coping with the fact problem. Although it sounds odd, the biggest problem with nonfiction is that the facts can get in the way. If you try to write a paragraph comparing Albert Einstein with Bozo the Clown, you will quickly discover that the only thing they have in common is the hairdo. Failing that, you could switch gears and try to contrast the two, but the differences are so obvious that the result may be dull. Bozo works in a circus whereas Einstein worked at a university. Who cares? The fact problem is easy to spot with this silly example, but in real life, fact problems are not so obvious.

Nonfiction writing is highly structured, but finding a suitable structure for the material is challenging. You can't just pick an arbitrary design because, to a certain extent the material dictates the design, as do the prewriting choices such as the purpose and the ideal reader. Consider the classic academic essay we all learned in school:

Introduction
First sentence stating thesis in broad terms.
Second sentence narrowing viewpoint and
leading into body.

Body
Three to five paragraphs, supporting or explaining
or defining thesis.

Conclusion
One sentence explaining how the thesis has been supported
or explained by the body.
Second sentence tying this piece to broader themes.

The Classic Academic Essay.

The design is like a classical Greek building, with the opening and conclusion framing the body of three to five gracefully balanced points. It seems so simple that one can be easily fooled into thinking it can handle almost any topic. It can't. Try to accurately describe, say, an automobile accident using this design. It is almost impossible to maintain the structure without distorting the facts. The only way to learn to match structure to material is to learn various possible designs and then to practice using them with different kinds of materials until one develops an intuitive feeling for which sorts of information might work best in what sorts of designs.

When giving nonfiction writing assignments, sometimes the material takes precedence and sometimes the writing takes precedence. If your main goal is teaching students how to write, as opposed to teaching them to master the subject they are writing about, you might want to adopt one of our strategies.

1. Provide the facts.

    This can be especially helpful for young students or those who are struggling to write. Make writing as easy as possible. Give them five points of comparison and ask them to write a comparison in their own words using two of those points. Draft a topic sentence for them initially. Use the "Research Strategy" (Chapter 2, Activity 4) to develop the research pointers they need so they have plenty of information. Use "Topics and Sluglines" (Activity 1) to help students organize their facts.

2. Use fiction first.

    Some nonfiction techniques don't work well with fiction, but many do. There is no reason students can't make up the facts they need for a fictional version.

3. Use familiar topics that don't require much research.

    Sixth- and seventh-graders enjoy writing about their families and their pets. Most students enjoy writing television or movie reviews or reporting on the latest basketball game.

4. Show them the tried-and-true methods.

    Write a detailed outline, keeping the techniques or a design in mind, then ask the students to write a paragraph based on your outline. Or, write a trial draft and have the students cut it apart, and tape it together into the best possible design, doing additional research if needed. (See Activity 2.)

5. Frame Paragraphs as Models

    Use a strategy called a framed paragraph to help model different patterns or designs in writing. (See Chapter 2, Activity 11 for a listing of different common designs.) Below is an example of a framed paragraph providing a topic sentence, transitions, and parts of a conclusion.

EXAMPLE

Even though box turtles and snapping turtles are in the same family, there are several

differences that you might want to consider before choosing one as a pet. Box turtles

live _____ while snapping turtles live _____ .

Another thing to consider is food. Box turtles eat _____.

Snapping turtles eat _____. Perhaps the most

important difference is their temperament. Box turtles are _____

_____ while snapping turtles are

_____ . Before choosing one of these turtles as a

pet, take _____ , _____ , and _____ into consideration.

If students struggle with this, try providing graphic organizers and examples that give them the information they need to plug into the framed paragraph. For example, when teaching students to write a comparison piece, start by giving them a diagram showing the overlapping characteristics that they can then plug into the framed paragraph.

EXAMPLE

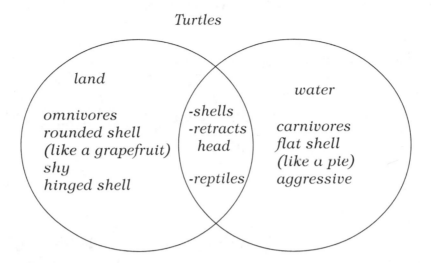

Turtles

land

omnivores
rounded shell
(like a grapefruit)
shy
hinged shell

-shells
-retracts
head

-reptiles

water

carnivores
flat shell
(like a pie)
aggressive

Keep repeating this type of modeling with the same design but different subjects, then move to a new design and try it with several different subjects. Once students are plugging their information into several different designs with confidence, move on to writing paragraphs with less help.

PART 1:
WRITING PARAGRAPHS

A technique may cover several paragraphs or a part of a paragraph. Ultimately, though, writing nonfiction is writing paragraphs, so the two activities included in this chapter focus on the paragraph. We use them again and again to give students practice with writing the paragraph. You can use the techniques (following the activities) to focus on specific parts of the paragraph. Once students are comfortable with writing one paragraph, have them attempt two paragraphs, then two paragraphs with an opening statement, and so forth. (See Chapter 3, Activity 6, for ideas on opening statements.)

Activity 1:
Topics and Sluglines

~ Knowledge is of two kinds. We know a
subject ourselves, or we know where we
can find information upon it.

—Samuel Johnson

If there is any student activity most used by professional writers, it is this one, or at least some version of this one. Sluglines make it easy to see what your main idea is and what supporting details you have to work with, without getting lost in the detail.

Sluglines—short phrases that describe details, definitions, or descriptions in less than five words. Using them makes it easy to see what the main idea is and what supporting details the writer has to work with. We have students use topics to describe the topic of the paragraph and sluglines to describe and organize the details under that topic.

Teach students to keep sluglines short and not usually complete sentences. As they gather and organize information, sluglines help students write the information in their own words rather than copying chunks of material.

We have students read their topics and sluglines to their editing groups, time permitting. The group discussion gives them an opportunity to think through and explain the relationships between the ideas represented by their sluglines before they write and this helps them write in their own words.

Instructions to Students

When writing nonfiction, each paragraph has one main idea that you use to write the topic sentence. Beneath that main idea, you have ideas, facts, examples, and so forth that support the main idea. Today we are going to make a "Topics and Sluglines" chart, which will help you organize your main idea and your supporting details. Later, you will write one sentence for your main idea and one for each of your supporting ideas.

To make the chart, draw a line lengthwise down your paper to create two columns; the left-hand column should be one-third the width of the paper, the right-hand column two-thirds. You will write the topic for your paragraph in the left-hand column and sluglines for your specifics—your supporting points—in the right-hand column.

Let's do them one at a time. In the left-hand column, write down your main idea for the paragraph. A "topic" is a few words that express your main idea for a paragraph or the main idea for a piece of writing such as a report or an article.

EXAMPLES

Hot-Air Balloons Can Cross the Atlantic Ocean

Polar Bears Are Like Other Bears

Carving a Walking Stick

Types of Turtles

Sluglines are short, usually three- to five-word phrases, that summarize an idea, a fact, a story, or an example. In the right-hand column, write down one slugline for each supporting idea—fact, example, and so on. You can use books from the library to find specifics for sluglines, but don't copy. Write down just a few words, even just one word. You need enough words to help you remember what you want to discuss in a supporting statement later, but not so many words that you are copying your source. (Optional: When you are done, you can read your chart out loud to a member of your writing group and explain what your topics and sluglines mean in your own words. When you are writing your sluglines, imagine what you might say to your group.)

EXAMPLES

TOPICS	SLUGLINES
Polar bears are like other bears	-solitary animals
	-have 1-2 cubs each year
	-hibernate through winter
	-cubs raised by mother
	-unpredictable reaction to humans, sometimes dangerous

Topics and Sluglines Chart for One Paragraph.

TOPICS	SLUGLINES
Main: How to Carve a Walking Stick	-old-fashioned entertainment
Paragraph #1: choose the right wood	-soft for carving -knots and swirls for beauty -right length for walking

Paragraph #2: use the proper tools	-carving tools
	  chisels, knives, saws
	-sanding tools
	  sandpaper, sanding
	  wheels, sanding spoons
	-safety first
	  goggles, gloves

Topics and Sluglines Chart for Two Paragraphs.

Notice in our second example that we show two topics beneath the main topic—each supporting the main topic. Beneath our sluglines, we listed specific examples and facts that supported our sluglines. We found these facts and examples by doing research and, wherever possible, wrote them in very brief phrases—much like sluglines.

Activity 2:
The Paragraph Puzzle[1]

> ～Information's pretty thin stuff, unless mixed with experience.
>
> —Clarence Day

This is a great activity for helping students with nonfiction writing, where organizing ideas is so much a part of the writing process.

Students write their sentences on strips of paper—one sentence per strip—and put the paragraph puzzle together by putting the strips together. It's a backwards version of the old tried and true "cut and paste" the paragraph used to revise. Aumen and Greiner have further refined this process by color coding the strips so that the topic sentence is always one color, supporting details another, transitions still another, and the concluding sentence matches the topic sentence.

To prepare sets of paragraph strips, here's what you will need:

1 topic sentence (transition)—green

3 supporting sentences—yellow

1 closing sentence (transition)—blue

2 transition sentences—pink

1 Vis-à-Vis™ dry erase pen

cloth for wiping off the puzzle pieces

If you have a class of thirty students, you will need to make at least ten sets of these paragraph strips.

Because this activity lends itself well to many situations, try making sentence strips out of laminated poster board (3 x 36-inch strips) with magnetic strips glued on the back, cut apart colored transparencies for whole-class work on an overhead projector, or cut strips out of colored paper for individual work. The important thing to remember is to keep the colors consistent for each kind of sentence—topic sentence, supporting sentence, transition sentence, and concluding sentence.

We begin teaching students to organize their paragraphs by using the large poster board strips and providing each group of three students with a "Topics and Sluglines Chart" (Activity 1), so they have an idea what to write for the sentences. The groups write one sentence on each strip: a topic sentence on the green, supporting sentences on the yellow, and so forth. Once they have the sentences written, they use the strips on the magnetic blackboard to arrange and rearrange their sentences to make their paragraphs, rewriting as necessary to make the sentences fit together.

---

1. We'd like to thank Alice Griener and Maureen Aumen for this wonderful activity. They teach a writing class, "Expository Writing and Reading." Maureen teaches in Cherry Creek Schools in Aurora, Colorado, and Alice is a Chapter I teacher at West Middle School in Aurora, Colorado.

Instructions to Students

Today we are going to work on a "Paragraph Puzzle." You will be working in groups of three. Each group will get a set of puzzle pieces, a piece of paper with topics and sluglines, and an erasable marker.

You will write one sentence on each strip.

Put your puzzle strips together to make a paragraph by sticking them on the chalkboard. Read aloud your paragraph and rearrange the puzzle strips until the organization makes sense and writing flows well. Erase parts of sentences and rewrite as necessary.

The important thing to remember about a paragraph, any paragraph, is that everything in a paragraph is about one main idea. If you are writing a piece, for example, about raising turtles as pets, you might have three paragraphs, one about what kind of housing they need, one about what kind of food they need, and one about what kind of care they need. The main idea for the first paragraph is turtle houses. Don't write about other subjects, such as turtle food, in this paragraph, although you might include something about where to put the food in a turtle's house. When you put your puzzle strips together, the first thing you want to do is to throw out or rewrite any sentences that don't fit in that paragraph.

The first sentence you are going to write on one of the green puzzle pieces is the topic sentence. The topic sentence expresses the main idea of the paragraph, for example, turtle houses. You might write, "The type of house you choose for your turtle will depend on the type of turtle you own" or "There are four basic kinds of homes for pet turtles."

The other sentences in your paragraph support your main idea with specifics. For example, if your topic sentence is "There are four kinds of homes for pet turtles" your supporting sentences will tell your reader what kinds of homes there are and, perhaps why. If your topic sentence is "The type of home you choose for your turtle depends on the type of turtle you own," your supporting sentences will explain which types of turtles need which types of homes, and perhaps, why. Use information from the sluglines part of your topics and sluglines chart to write supporting sentences on the yellow puzzle strips. Today, we want you to write at least three supporting sentences, but you may write as many supporting sentences as you wish.

The last sentence of the paragraph wraps up the paragraph in some way. It may also lead into the next paragraph. It is called the closing sentence or conclusion. It goes on a blue strip. For example, to conclude a paragraph on housing pet turtles, you might say "Knowing what type of housing turtles need will help you decide what type of turtle to buy as a pet."

A sentence that leads from one thing to another, such as from one paragraph to the next or from one part of a paragraph to the next is called a transition. Write transition sentences on pink puzzle strips.

When you have more than one paragraph in a story or report, opening and closing sentences can also be transitions—in fact, they usually are. For example, if the article on pet turtles had a second paragraph on food, the conclusion for the first paragraph on turtle houses might say, "Now that you know which kinds of houses to buy or build for your turtle, you need to know how to feed it." This sentence closes the paragraph on houses, so it is a conclusion. It also leads into the next paragraph on food, so it is a transition. When the sentence you are working on is both a conclusion and a transition or an opening and a transition, put the sentence on a green puzzle strip for openings or a blue puzzle piece for conclusions.

Now, put your puzzle strips together to make a paragraph. Read it out loud. Does it make sense? Try rearranging your sentences. Does it make more sense or sound better? You can also erase and rewrite any sentences or parts of sentences you want. Does every sentence fit with your main idea? If not, take out those that don't. Write another sentence to replace the one you took out. Keep rearranging and rewriting until it makes sense and fits together. When you are all done, copy the final paragraph onto a piece of paper for final storage in your portfolio.

Additional Notes to Teachers

- Most of the variety in the game comes from trying different topics, different techniques, and so forth. You can also add variety by playing the game in different ways. For example, pass out yellow puzzle strips to each student. Assign a topic, presumably one that students have been studying together. Then, ask them each to write on their yellow puzzle pieces a specific statement about that topic. Afterwards, have the students in each group put their statements together, write a topic sentence to connect the supporting sentences together, rewrite the supporting sentences as necessary, and add a closing sentence.

- Have students write supporting sentences using some of the nonfiction techniques, such as comparison or definition.

- *Patience* is the watchword. They won't "get it," as students would say, for a while, but eventually, you will see improvements in their writing, sometimes quite dramatic. In the meantime, though, be patient.

PART 2:
A CATALOG OF NONFICTION TECHNIQUES

Teaching the Techniques

One of the best ways to avoid certain pitfalls of teaching nonfiction is to teach techniques. It is actually a lot easier to explain how to write an anecdote or an example than how to structure a paragraph. Then students can use anecdotes and examples to help them write supporting statements in their paragraphs.

Once students begin to understand a few techniques, it is easier to tackle paragraphs. We teach a little technique, practice paragraphs awhile, then write leads, write a little nonfiction, then a little fiction. Once students have written a few good paragraphs, we work on writing pieces with several paragraphs, using either "Topics and Sluglines" (Activity 1) or "The Design" (Chapter 2, Activity 11) to develop a plan.

Anecdotes

Explanation

When writers present examples, they sometimes write them as thumbnail stories called anecdotes. People like reading stories, even pint-sized stories. Anecdotes written with fiction techniques, such as dialogue or action, are sometimes called fictional anecdotes, but the facts of the little story are real. Some short magazine articles are all anecdotes, nothing else.

EXAMPLES

When Rasila decided to buy a dog, she spent several hours debating which set of floppy ears and brown eyes seemed most appealing before a smart pet store owner set her straight. Selecting the breed to match the owner's lifestyle is important, he explained, because personality traits bred into a dog cannot be trained out of it.

Writers become attached to their pens. My favorite word weapon is the cheap cartridge fountain pen. The cheap ones are better than the expensive ones, incidentally. They flow more easily with the ideas. The only problem is replacing them when they gum up. *I spent four hours tracking one down yesterday. I finally found one—just one—buried at the bottom of a rack of designer felt-tips and ball-points. Ominously, some of the stores no longer carried fountain pens.* If the cheap fountain pen follows the dinosaur into extinction, I may be next.

Tricks of the Trade

◆ Anecdotes must be short and punchy. Try the three-sentence technique: The first sets up the story, the second contains a crisis, the third leads into the next section with a solution. Television advertisements use this constantly. (A word of warning: When you use the three-sentence technique, make sure it doesn't sound like you are selling slicers and dicers for $29.95.)

EXAMPLE

First Sentence—Setup: I could never get grass stains out of the children's clothes.

Second Sentence—Crisis: One day, Jimmy's teacher sent him home from school to get a clean shirt.

Third Sentence—Solution: Then I discovered Super Sudso Detergent.

Next Sentence: Yessiree, folks, Super Sudso gets out the toughest stains.

Comparison and Contrast

Explanation

Comparison is a description of how things are similar, whereas *contrast* is a description of how things are different. Often, they are discussed together, but more often they are discussed separately because things with a lot of similarities don't tend to have as many differences. The best way to write a comparison or contrast is to make a list of the similarities and differences; then, choose one or the other to emphasize. For example, write a comparison covering several similarities, and use just one point of contrast to add interest or color.

You can write comparisons or contrasts at different levels: an entire piece, one paragraph, or one sentence. You can also write mini-comparisons, which are just part of a sentence, called similes and metaphors.

EXAMPLES

Paragraph

Polar bears are like most other bears. Like other bears, they are solitary animals, meeting other bears only a few times a year, such as for mating or when waiting for the ice to break. They, too, hibernate in winter, digging themselves snow caves. During the winter hibernation, mother bears give birth to their young, usually one or two cubs. Their newborn cubs spend the winter growing larger and stronger before emerging in spring. Mother polar bears, like all mother bears, raise their cubs alone. Indeed, male bears often kill cubs, and polar bear males are especially dangerous to cubs. Unlike the North American black bears and brown bears, polar bears do not eat berries and fruit. There are no berries and fruit at the polar ice caps, so polar bears live exclusively on fish and sea lions. Like their bear cousins, however, polar bears have unpredictable, often dangerous reactions to humans.

Sentence

Polar bears, like most other bears, are solitary animals, bear few young, hibernate in winter, and have a grumpy attitude towards people.

Mini-Comparisons

Similes and metaphors can be anywhere from one to several words in length. (Many times, similes and metaphors are poetic, comparing two things that are not alike at all.)

Similes

In a simile, the comparison is stated using the word *like* or *as*.

Jake was *as grumpy as a hungry bear*.

I want to be *as independent as a polar bear*.

The neighbor's dog, Lulu, had fur *like a polar bear*.

The six-year old acted *like a monkey* at the wedding.

My dog serves *as the household vacuum cleaner*, suctioning up every crumb that drops on the floor.

Metaphors

In a metaphor, the comparison is not stated using the word *like* or *as*.

The neighbor's dog, Lulu, *had the fur of a polar bear*.

The six-year-old *was a monkey* at the wedding.

My dog *vacuums the house, suctioning up* every crumb that drops on the floor.

My dog *is a vacuum*.

Extended metaphors and similes are called analogies. You might, for example, compare cities to ant colonies, or the human heart to a water pump, or traffic to water. Usually, analogies are about a paragraph long, with a topic sentence making the comparison (e.g., "Ant colonies and cities are alike in many ways") and the supporting sentences showing how the two things are alike.

It helps to have a few words and phrases for writing comparisons and contrasts.

Comparisons	Contrasts
like	unlike
as	not as
by comparison	by contrast or whereas
seems like, sounds like,	the reverse of, or mirror image of looks like, tastes like
similar	opposite
the same as	different from, dissimilar
resemble	differ
take after	stand apart
remind one of	run counter to
bring to mind	on the other hand
approximate	distinct, distinguished from
come close to	diverge
come near	depart from
duplicate	separate, differentiate
parallel	poles apart, at opposite ends
match	not matched
simulate	dissimilar, dissimulate
imitate	avoid, set oneself (or it) apart from

It is easy to spot comparisons and contrasts while reading, and they come up naturally in conversation all the time; however, it is not always easy to decide what to compare or contrast when you want to write. Here are some ideas:

1. How things look (shape, size, color, texture, proportions)
2. Attitudes or opinions of different people
3. Points of view (e.g., teachers vs. students, coaches vs. athletes, truck drivers vs. automobile drivers)
4. Before and after (e.g., a snowstorm or earthquake, a learning experience, a trip, summer vacation)
5. How things are done (e.g., styles of playing a sport, beginners vs. experts, cooking vs. writing)
6. How things work (e.g., engines vs. windpower, engine vs. human heart, computer vs. brain, e-mail vs. postal mail)

7. Things in the natural world: plants, animals, minerals, viruses, cells, plankton, protozoa (dogs vs. cats, bacteria vs. plankton, volcanic vs. sedimentary)

8. Cycles (e.g., daytime vs. nighttime, spring vs. fall)

9. People (e.g., brothers vs. sisters; friends; teachers; characters in movies and books)

10. Wacky comparisons of things that aren't really similar (e.g., getting lost on purpose vs. getting lost by accident, anteaters vs. disk jockeys) or contrasts of things that aren't really different (cats that nap vs. cats that fight)

Tricks of the Trade

♦ Don't try to balance your points of comparison or contrast, such as listing three points of comparison and three points of contrast. The real world is rarely so balanced, and trying to balance the world in writing will tend to distort the facts.

♦ Pick the most interesting points, rather than the most points. It's better to fully describe one interesting point of comparison or contrast than to make a laundry list of dull points.

♦ Don't overwork your analogies. Analogies are fun to write and do help you understand things in ways you wouldn't without the analogy, but do keep in mind that it is only an analogy, and no analogy is perfect. Yes, the computer *is* like a human brain, but only up to a point. After that, a computer is not at all like a human brain; come to think of it, you could write an entire piece showing how it is not at all like a human brain—up to a point.

Conclusions

Explanation

The conclusion is the end of a fictional story or nonfiction piece. It wraps up the fictional story or sums up the points in a nonfiction piece.

The most important thing to understand before writing your conclusion is the purpose of your piece. When you have accomplished your purpose, stop. That's the conclusion, the end. If you are giving your opinion of a movie, you have reached the end when you have given your opinion. If you are describing the lifestyle of the polar bear, stop when you have nothing else new to tell your reader.

Tricks of the Trade

♦ There are a few tricks to creating a sense of finality in the last sentence. If you have been talking in detail about the daily life of the polar bear, pull the camera back, so to speak, and describe the polar bear in a little bit broader context, such as "the King of the Arctic." Similarly, if you are describing how you liked particular scenes and characters in a movie, giving your opinion of this movie compared to others of the same genre or others released this year paints a little bit broader picture and creates a sense of finality. Another way to do this is to connect the last sentence to the first sentence by repeating a key word or expressing the main idea in a different way. For example, "Although the polar bear is like other bears in many ways, it is the only King of the Arctic.

◆ Don't write "in conclusion" and then try to write a concluding sentence. It is often repetitive and it always sounds odd. When you have accomplished your purpose, stop and read aloud the last sentence. Does it sound like the end? If you crossed it out, would it make a difference to your reader? If not, cross it out and read the next to last sentence. Does this sentence sound like the end? What to we mean by "sound like the end"? Well, "And they lived happily ever after" sounds like the end of a story. "Despite a few problems, it was the best movie I have seen this year" sounds like an end of an opinion piece. "For many people, the best bear is the polar bear" sounds like the end of an essay about polar bears. Practice listening to the last sentence for that feeling of finality.

◆ If you don't know how to end your piece, write down the purpose of the piece so that you have it clearly in mind. What sentences don't match your purpose? (You might want to cross them out.) At what point do you accomplish your purpose? If you haven't done that yet, keep writing until you do. Then stop and read aloud the last sentence.

Definition

Explanation

A definition is a sentence or a paragraph (or several paragraphs) that explain what a word or a phrase means. Of course, a dictionary is a book of definitions, but almost all nonfiction writing, especially technical and scientific writing, uses definitions.

Definitions can be short or long, formal or informal, real or imaginary.

EXAMPLES

Formal

A central processing unit (CPU) is the heart of a computer. A computer program is a list of instructions telling the CPU what to do. The CPU only really understands "on" or "off," which it understands as 0 or 1. This is called binary code. Computer programmers used to write their programs in binary code, but could only read it with difficulty. To overcome the problem, computer programmers wrote programs that translate instructions written in binary code languages into a little more like human language. These programs are called compilers.

Informal

My automobile is my central processing unit. It is a machine that works in ways I don't understand, but my entire life depends on it.

Imaginary

(nonfiction) A camel is a horse that was designed by committee.

(fiction) Jona looked forward to Squallender, the spring holiday most popular in Medocal.

Tricks of the Trade

◆ Good definitions are mostly hard work. Be prepared to revise, read it to friends and strangers, revise, and then revise again.

◆ As a rule of thumb, write the definitions first. That way you will use them consistently all the way through the story or the nonfiction piece.

◆ Look up words in the dictionary—or rather, at least three different dictionaries. Then write your own definition in your own words. Seeing the differences among three dictionaries will help you formulate your own approach.

Division and Classification

Explanation

Division is an explanation or description in which the writer splits something into parts. Classification is similar, except the writer sorts different things into categories.

EXAMPLES

Division: There are three main parts to an automobile: the engine, the drive train, and the body.

Division (funny version): There are four main parts to an automobile: the engine, the drive train, the body, and the maniac who owns it.

Classification: Two main groups of dinosaurs evolved early in dinosaur history: the Saurischians, or lizard-hipped dinosaurs, and the Ornithischians, or bird-hipped dinosaurs. *Tyrannosaurus rex* is a Saurischian, while *Stegosaurus ungulatus* is an Ornithischian.

Classification (funny version): I only eat three kinds of health food: ice cream, potato chips, and bacon.

Like comparisons and contrasts, divisions and classifications can be written as entire pieces, paragraphs, sentences, or parts of sentences. To begin, try things with just two classifications: tall or short, fast or slow, near or far, or having some characteristic or not, such as blond-haired or not, tomato-based or not, clean or not, smelly or not.

Divisions and classifications are almost always combined with an explanation, example, definition, or description to make a paragraph. Otherwise, you only have a list.

It helps to know how to punctuate division and classification sentences.

EXAMPLES

There are three colors in the American flag: red, white, and blue.

The study showed three reasons for endangered species:

1. loss of habitat

2. poaching

3. low reproduction

The study showed three reasons for endangered species: loss of habitat, poaching, and low reproduction.

The study showed three reasons for endangered species: a steady loss of habitat, especially due to logging; high rates of poaching in areas critical to the species; and low reproduction rates, sometimes made worse by pesticides.

Tricks of the Trade

♦ If you want to see examples of classification and division, read this book! It's built around dividing and classifying the rather amorphous writing process to make it more concrete and accessible.

♦ Division and classification sounds dreadfully dull, so don't forget humor. Division and classification are favorites of humor writers. We like to introduce this idea with a funny column by outdoor writer Patrick F. McManus called "Modified Stationary Panic," from *A Fine and Pleasant Misery.* He explains that there are many different kinds of panic among those lost in the wilderness, including "group panics" and "full-bore-linear panics," but the one he recommends is "modified stationary panic." He provides his own hilarious definitions and examples.

Examples

Explanation

Examples are the life of the nonfiction party. They make dull ideas come alive. "Not all beautiful trees make good street trees" is pretty ho-hum without examples.

EXAMPLE

Not all beautiful trees make good street trees. The London plane's iron roots can shred a cement sidewalk or snap a steel water main. Dutch elm disease has nearly wiped out the elm, a popular street tree at the turn of the century. Street trees can't be maintenance headaches or prone to disease. They must grow quickly to a size that can withstand car exhaust and pedestrian vandalism. Their branches should not bat pedestrians in the face or rain sticky sap on parked cars. That's a lot to ask of a tree.

You can string examples together, as in the example above, or you can use one good example to make your point.

EXAMPLE

Not all beautiful trees make good street trees. At the turn of the century, elm trees were planted along boulevards and city squares in towns all across the United States. In the 1960s, Dutch elm disease—a virus that infects and kills elms—began to spread from east to west, stripping city after city of its elegant elms. In the 1980s, it picked many of Denver's boulevards clean and pushed on towards San Francisco.

Tricks of the Trade

+ Deciding how you want to present your example will help you write it. Think of an example as being one of three types: the short example, the extended example, or the storylike example.

EXAMPLES

Short: Elms are killed by Dutch elm disease.

Extended: Elms are killed by Dutch elm disease. By the 1980s, this virus had destroyed many of the elms in the United States.

Storylike: (See the examples of street trees, above.)

+ You can use two or three long examples. If, however, you have told a story in the first example that you use, be sure to tell stories of about the same length for the other examples. Otherwise, the later examples will seem incomplete and tacked on to the first example.

+ Keep together the same kinds of examples. All the examples in the first example of street trees, above, illustrate the point, but the examples include specific trees, bad characteristics, and good characteristics, presented in groups.

+ One specialized example is the list. It's used in textbooks and reference books to quickly present a large number of examples in a way that is easy to read.

EXAMPLE

Not all beautiful trees make good street trees. City arborists should not include the following trees on their lists of approved trees:

elms

London planes

large pines with heavy sap

weeping willows

+ Introduce examples with "for example" or "such as" if it might not be clear to your reader that you are giving an example.

EXAMPLES

Not all beautiful trees make good street trees. The elm, for example, is gorgeous, but a poor choice for a street tree.

Trees such as the elm, the London plane, and the weeping willow should not be used as street trees.

Transitions

(See also Chapter 5.)

Explanation

A transition is the technique in writing that concerns moving from one chapter to the next, from one section to the next, from one paragraph to the next, from one sentence to the next. Think of a transition as a little bridge that carries your reader from one part of the writing to another. Transitions themselves can vary in length. A transition can be a paragraph, a sentence, or just a word or two that leads the reader forward. A leader (see Chapter 3, Activity 6) is really just a transitional sentence leading from the hook into the main body of the piece.

Transitions are one of the most difficult parts of writing, in fiction as well as nonfiction. Not only do you need to move from one section or paragraph to another, you need to do so clearly so that you do not lose the reader in the process. Further, you want to do so unobtrusively, using as few words as possible. There are as many ways to make transitions as there are writers. Below are four useful methods.

1. Repeat a key term before and after the move.

EXAMPLE

(A transition between two paragraphs using the key term *polar bear*. The transition is bold italic.)

People have for many years been fascinated by the *polar bear*, but now scientists are most interested in their survival. . . .
Polar Bears require large territories, give birth to few young, and do not mix well with civilization.

Instead of repeating the key term, you can use a similar word or phrase (e.g., "this magnificent animal" or "the white bear of the Arctic").

2. Set up a transition before making it. The setup can come much earlier in the piece or just before the transition.

EXAMPLE

(A nonfiction transition to a new section. The transition is bold italic.)

James *Madison* kept *notes* of the constitutional convention, *contributing to our present understanding of the constitution as much as the document itself.* . . .
Madison's notes are the most complete minutes of the convention. The official secretary found keeping track of the debates too difficult, and the convention was closed to the press.

3. There are many words that help writers make transitions. They can be used anywhere in the transitional sentence, but they are usually used toward the beginning. A starter list follows.

<u>Transitional Words and Phrases</u>

TRANSITIONS OF TIME

after	later
after that	many years (days, months, etc.) later
afterward	next
all the time	the next day
all through	on Monday
as long as	once
as yet	over ("over five years")
at the time	recently (currently)
before	still
by the time	that morning (afternoon, evening, etc.)
during	this wasn't the first time . . . once before
the first time, the last time	throughout
the first time . . . the next time	until
for ("for the next five years")	up to this point
in the meantime	when
just as	while

TRANSITIONS OF PLACE

At the [place]

In [place]

Foreshadow the change of place by having a character anticipate going there.

EXAMPLE
(The transition is bold italic.)

John knew *Trenton* was a rough town. He had never been there and wasn't looking forward to it. . . .
The streets of Trenton were covered with wet litter. John walked down one alley.

Remember that a change of place usually involves some change of time as well, so you might need a transition of time.

TRANSITIONS TO CONTRASTING IDEAS OR DESCRIPTIONS

although

_____ believe(s) that . . . _____ believe(s) that

but, yet, still

by contrast

despite

either . . . or

even though

however

in that case . . . but in this case

ironically (happily, tragically, or other introductory phrases)

neither . . . nor

nonetheless, nevertheless

normally, usually

on the one hand . . . on the other hand

on the one side . . . on the other side

TRANSITIONS TO SUPPORTING IDEAS OR DESCRIPTIONS

according to

better yet

even better

even worse

finally

first . . . second . . . third

for example

in addition to

in the first place . . . furthermore . . . moreover

more important than _____ is (was) _____

moreover

one of the

such as

what's more

worse yet

(Pagination of paragraphs or lists can also be used as transitional devices.)

WRAPPING UP

Sometimes these transitions are useful, but try to conclude without them, especially without "in conclusion."

as a result	owing to
for these reasons	therefore
in conclusion	thus
in summary, to summarize	ultimately

Some of these transitional words can become a crutch for the lazy writer. If your work is loaded with *moreover*s, *therefore*s, and *thus*es, *try making transitions by repeating key words until you break the habit.*

Tricks of the Trade

* If your rough draft of a piece seems confusing or poorly organized, check your transitions before doing anything else. Clumsy or confusing transitions can make pieces that are well organized seem disorganized.

* It is easy to fall into the habit of using the same transition method for every piece even though another method might work better. Try writing transitions using several different methods until you feel comfortable with a variety of methods. The better you get at using a variety of transitions, the easier writing will become.

Fiction Workshop

MEANS

> If you're a singer, you lose your voice. A baseball player loses his arm. A writer gets more knowledge, and if he's good, the older he gets the better he writes.
>
> —Mickey Spillane

INTRODUCTION

If you want your students to develop fluency, confidence, the ability to write longer pieces, and a sense of using good details, a discussion of fiction techniques is the place to begin. It is easier to teach some of the more difficult, technical aspects of writing, such as transitions, in fiction than nonfiction. Once students can comfortably move from one time or place to the next by connecting scenes with transitions, moving from one idea to the next in nonfiction (see Chapter 4) is much easier.

In Part 1, we present one of our favorite writing activity: "Weaving Scenes." You can use it again and again for a hundred different lessons; it always works and never grows stale. Teachers from fourth grade to college have reported success with this activity. As presented here, "Weaving the Scenes" introduces action, dialogue, introspection, and description, but it can be used as a template—combined with the activity "Follow the Leader" (Chapter 3, Activity 8)—to teach any fiction technique. Use our examples or those you find all around you, but don't be too picky. If an example might help students develop a feel for the pace and the level of detail they want to achieve, use it.

We frequently begin a fiction workshop by teaching narrative technique, asking students to write the entire story in narrative first. Narrative writing is short and easy to read as a whole. Then we have students choose sentences from their narrative and expand them by weaving in action and dialogue, and by using the other fiction techniques. Students love this; it's a real thrill for them to see their writing expand—like popcorn almost. They love the way their stories begin to sound more adult.

Of note, the hard part of fiction is ending the story. If students can't find a good end to the story, don't worry about it. Have them write the story in scenes, pursing one scene after another. They may find the ending somewhere in the writing. They may think of an ending later. In the meantime, they will have learned a lot about writing, even if they never find a good ending. For students who can never seem to find an ending, suggest that they try nonfiction, in which endings are a little easier to write. They may find that they prefer nonfiction. Most adult writers develop a preference for either fiction or nonfiction; students are no different.

Part 2, "A Catalog of Fiction Techniques," presents an alphabetical listing of techniques— action, description, dialogue, flashback, foreshadowing, introspection, narrative, and transitions— each with an explanation, examples, and "Tricks of the Trade" (tips for using the technique). Although most of the techniques covered in this chapter are basic, foreshadowing is more advanced. We have included discussion of foreshadowing partly because it is so much fun, partly because students begin to develop an interest in the craft of writing when they try foreshadowing. Also, it helps them learn how to use transitions.

PART 1:
THE SCENE

The scene is the fundamental building block of fiction. This differs from nonfiction where the paragraph, not the section, is the fundamental building block. In part 1 we have one activity, "Weaving Scenes," that we use to introduce students to all the fictional techniques. This activity takes a little time to explain the meaning of action, dialogue, and so forth, but it produces instant improvements in the students' writing that they can see. If you want to get your students charged up about writing and learning writing techniques, try "Weaving Scenes."

Activity 1:
Weaving Scenes

～Personally, I would sooner have written *Alice in Wonderland* than the whole *Encyclopaedia Britannica*.

—Stephen Leacock

Nature built sixth- and seventh-graders to write fiction. This activity, combined with a few of the activities in Chapter 3, such as Activity 3, "Braindancing and Downhilling" or Activity 8 "Follow the Leader" will help twelve- to fifteen-year-olds write fiction. Once students have written two or three scenes for a story, have them use transitions to hook together the scenes.

Instructions for Students

You can't write fiction without scenes, any more than you can build a house without wood, bricks, and cement. Despite the importance of scenes, many writers struggle when asked to exactly define *scene*. A scene is just one piece of a story. Some people define it as "a portion of a story that takes place at the same time and same place." That's true, but our favorite definition for *scene* is "the part of a story where the writer shows the reader what happens in the story, as opposed to telling the reader what happens." This definition comes from a famous rule of thumb among writers: "Show; don't tell."

When you tell the story, you use a type of writing called narrative. A little narrative goes a long way. If you use too much, though, the story becomes a long, boring string of "and then's."

EXAMPLE

John picked Bob up at the airport, and then John took Bob home, and then Bob said he was tired from his trip, so then John went home and Bob went to bed.

To write this short story in scenes, the writer weaves together action, dialogue, introspection, and description to show John at the airport, anxiously scanning the departure/arrival monitors to find the right flight, wondering if he got the wrong one, being jostled by other passengers. Don't be put off by the fancy sounding techniques. They are really quite simple, but you need to know a little bit about these techniques before you can use them to write your scenes:

- **Action** is what the characters do in a scene. It can be big actions ("George leaped from the burning building") or little actions ("George turned the key in the lock").

- **Dialogue** is what the characters say in a scene. One of the hardest things about dialogue is the punctuation. For now, just remember to begin a new paragraph each time a new character speaks, and to enclose the words the character says in quotation marks.

EXAMPLE

> Jason dashed through the kitchen, slammed the door behind him, and arrived panting in the living room. His sister, Mary, was curled up in the big chair reading a book.
>
> *"What do you want?"* she asked irritably.
>
> *"Oh,"* Jason replied, glancing over his shoulder, *"nothing really."*
>
> Mary glared at him. *"Don't bug me then."*
>
> *"I wasn't! I just—"*
>
> *"You were too. You are always bugging me,"* Mary flounced from the room, leaving Jason with his problem unsolved.

- **Introspection** is what the characters think in a scene. There are two ways to use introspection: As internal dialogue or as plain introspection. Internal dialogue presents the character's thoughts just like spoken dialogue using "thought" (or its synonyms such as "remembered" or "imagined") in place of "said" or its synonyms. Unlike internal dialogue, plain introspection does not use "thought" or its synonyms to present a character's thoughts. Plain introspection should be written only where it is obvious to the reader which character is thinking. The writer doesn't use such phrases as "he thought." Note: Don't use quotation marks for introspection.

EXAMPLES

Internal Dialogue

> Allen raced to the bus stop.
> *Oh no, he thought. I can't be late again. It's my third time.*

Plain Introspection

Allen raced to the bus stop. *He couldn't be late again. It was the third time.*

- **Description** shows how the setting and the characters look. The reader can't see them, so the writer must describe them—or at least describe two or three interesting details to help the reader imagine the place and the characters.

Today, we are going to learn an easy way to develop a simple, narrative sentence into a professional-sounding scene, so get out your writing notebook and a sharp pencil. Invent at least two characters and give them names. Imagine a place; any place will do.

Write a simple narrative sentence about what happens to these characters in that place. Keep it simple: "John told Mary he was mad" or "Susan and Julie did the dishes" provide plenty of action for a short scene. Assign each of your characters a mood; for example, happy, angry, patient, frustrated, frightened, or silly.

You may also want a starter sentence to help you get rolling. It's always easier to write when you are not beginning with a blank page. Try "Now that [character] was here in (on, at) [the place], he (she) . . ." Just fill in the name of one of your characters and the place. For example, "Now that Joe was here on the doorstep, he . . ." or "Now that Grumpie was here at the state fair, he . . ." Cross out your starter sentence when you finish the scene.

All set? Begin to weave your scene. Write what characters do (action) and say (dialogue). As you write, try to weave together the action and the dialogue: Write a little action, then a little dialogue, then a little more action, and so forth. Don't try to write perfectly. Just get it on paper, writing quickly and easily. A few minutes should be enough time to finish the scene. Write on every third line of the page to allow plenty of room for later additions.

EXAMPLE

Characters: Muskrat and Beaver

Place: Muskrat's kitchen

Starter Sentence: Now that Muskrat was here in his kitchen, he flung a glass into the dish rack.

Muskrat was angry.

Muskrat and Beaver did the dishes.

Beaver was frustrated.

~~Now that Muskrat was here in his kitchen, he . . .~~

~~The muskrat flung a glass into the dish rack~~

(Action is italic; the rest is dialogue.)

"I will never give another dinner party for the rest of my life," Muskrat announced flatly.

"You want everyone and everything to be just perfect," said Beaver. "Then you get mad and make people uncomfortable when they don't do exactly as you wish."

Beaver opened the kitchen drawer, searching for a towel with which to dry the dishes that Muskrat was throwing at the rack.

"Mallard put his elbows on the table and was a perfect slob," cried Muskrat. "And the rest of you were behaving like a pack of wild animals."

"Well," answered Beaver, "we are wild animals. What did you expect?"

Muskrat snorted. "That is no excuse for being uncivilized."

Action and dialogue go together. Too much action is confusing, whereas too much dialogue is boring. You can also think of action and dialogue as working together to paint the foreground of the scene—the part of the scene closest to the reader. Introspection and description, fill in the background. You need both foreground and background to show the full picture, so the next step is to weave the background into your scene.

Go through the scene and add a little description and introspection, here and there. This paints in the background, the description showing how things look, the introspection showing what the characters think. Add more action and dialogue if you need it.

There are a couple of tricks to writing description and introspection that may help you. Good description is detailed. You don't need to describe everything; just pick out two or three details and describe them accurately. Good description is also specific: "The sky was pink" is more interesting than "The sky was beautiful" because it is more specific. Use "German shepherd" or "springer spaniel" instead of "dog," and "daisy" or "lily" instead of "flower," for the same reason.

When you weave in the introspection, write the thoughts of just one of the characters in the scene. You can write thoughts for each character, but it is easier to stay with just one character's thoughts.

EXAMPLE

(Description is italic; introspection is bold; the rest is action and dialogue.)

Muskrat flung a glass into the dish rack. "I will never give another dinner party for the rest of my life," he announced flatly.

"You want everyone and everything to be just perfect," said Beaver. **He had enjoyed the party. Muskrat got so fussed up about such minor problems.** "Then you get mad and make people uncomfortable when they don't do exactly as you wish."

Beaver opened the kitchen drawer searching for a towel with which to dry the dishes that Muskrat was throwing at the rack. *Each drawer was a tidy reflection of its owner. The knives gleamed from careful rows, and the tins of vegetables and fruits were arranged by category. The kitchen towels were folded neatly in the bottom drawer, each embroidered with a saying. Beaver selected "Home Is Where the Heart Is."* **Perhaps Otter could have been more careful not to spill his grape juice on the carpet. But why have guests if they can't enjoy themselves?**

"Mallard put his elbows on the table and was a perfect slob," cried Muskrat. "And the rest of you were behaving like a pack of wild animals."

"Well," answered Beaver, "we are wild animals. What did you expect?"

Muskrat snorted. "That is no excuse for being uncivilized."

If you made a big mess adding in the introspection and description, recopy your scene, putting things in the proper order and making any improvements you wish. Read your scene to a friend. The introspection and the description fill out the scene and, suddenly, it sounds professional, just like the scenes you read in books.

Of course, you don't need to stop here. Weave in more bits of action, dialogue, description, and introspection until you think it sounds just right.

Additional Notes to Teachers

- ◆ Have students write a scene weaving together all four techniques in the first draft.

- ◆ Have students write description and introspection first, and add the action and dialogue in the second pass.

- ◆ Have students write at least one scene in which the characters are animals. For some reason, practice with animal characters teaches young writers how to write scenes that portray vivid, interesting human characters.

- ◆ Have students study the scenes in published fiction for ideas.

- ◆ Once your students feel comfortable weaving single scenes, tackle an entire story. Get them started by writing an outline using simple narrative sentences.

EXAMPLE

The animals have a dinner party at Muskrat's:

1. Muskrat and Beaver do the dishes.

2. Muskrat decides to sponsor an etiquette class.

3. The class is a disaster.

4. Muskrat invites the animals to dinner, telling them to go ahead and behave badly. He has given up his crusade. But now, the animals prefer to follow the rules of etiquette.

Have students weave a scene for each sentence and then hook together the scenes.

PART 2:
A CATALOG OF FICTION TECHNIQUES

Teaching the Techniques

To create a classroom activity based on a technique, use the explanation together with the activity "Follow the Leader" (Chapter 3, Activity 8) to introduce the technique, and then ask students to write a scene or section using the technique. Work one scene at a time. (By the way, don't ask that students use any particular technique in a complete story. The technique may not apply and they might wind up with all sorts of unexpected problems for themselves trying to use it in the story.)

Keep in mind that the distinction between fiction and nonfiction begins to break down at the level of technique. Almost all the so-called fiction techniques are used routinely in nonfiction, and most of the nonfiction techniques are used occasionally in fiction. Usually, we introduce fiction techniques by teaching students how to write a scene (see Activity 1). Then we introduce nonfiction techniques by teaching students how to write a section. Although description, action, and narrative are all used in nonfiction, it is usually easier for students to learn about them in the context of fiction.

A few tips on teaching technique: Cover a range of techniques quickly, rather than covering any one in depth. Slip in a technique here and there among other practice exercises, and keep your presentations quick and light. Beginning writers usually overdo a new technique; it's a natural part of learning. Knowing a little about a range of techniques helps students more than knowing a great deal about any one. Use the "Tricks of the Trade" as helpful points for follow-up discussions or for quick reference when students have editing questions.

Action

Explanation

Action is what the characters do in a scene, as opposed to dialogue, which is what characters say. Action can include big actions (e.g., "Alex jumped from the shed roof to the garden walk and ran to the front of the house") or little actions, sometimes called "business" (e.g., "Alex set his glass on the counter"). Too much action is hard to follow, so action is almost always woven together with dialogue, introspection, description, or narrative.

EXAMPLES

(Action is italic [our addition].)

> "You will go." *The milk-eyes looked through him to these, to the snow, to the line of blue that was the sky.* "You will go now."
> And there was such strength in his voice that Russel knew he must go. *He took the handlebar in one hand and pulled the hook, and the dogs surged away and Russel let them run without looking back.*
> —Gary Paulsen, *Dogsong*

> "Hullo," he said, beaming. "Where did you spring from? Come and have a warmer up at the Angel."
> *I nodded and walked beside him, shuffling on the thawing remains of the previous week's snow.*
> —Dick Francis, *Flying Finish*

Tricks of the Trade

• Your reader must be able to picture who is coming into and going out of the scene, and what the characters are doing. A little bit of business adds color and makes for an authentic scene. You don't need to write every move your characters make because readers have good imaginations.

• Beginners often try to add zip by adding adverbs. For example: "He walked quickly and quietly from the room." Be aware, though, that adverbs slow down the action. If you want to slow it down, fine. If you want to speed up the action, use a good, strong verb. For example: "He tiptoed from the room." Below is a starter list of strong verbs.

Walked Quickly		Walked Slowly	
blasted	jogged	ambled	roved
bolted	jumped	crawled	sauntered
bounced	loped	dawdled	shuffled
careened	raced	drifted	staggered
darted	ran	hiked	straggled
dashed	roared	hobbled	strolled
escaped	rushed	inched	teetered
fled	scampered	limped	toddled
flitted	scrambled	meandered	toured
gallivanted	scurried	minced	traversed
hastened	skipped	moseyed	trekked
hopped	skittered	prowled	wandered
hurried	speeded	rambled	wound
jaunted	tore	roamed	wobbled

If the strong verbs don't seem strong enough, try an unusual verb. For example: "He whispered away." "She screamed into the driveway."

♦ The word *suddenly*. What to do with all those suddenly's? Because it's an adverb, *suddenly* slows down the action just at the point it should speed up the action. Try deleting it. Or, try to foreshadow the sudden event.

EXAMPLE

Without Foreshadowing

Richard spread the newspaper on the dining room table. Suddenly, the tarantula pounced.

With Foreshadowing

Richard flushed away the crumbled tissue and the spider. Big spider, he chuckled. Maria wouldn't know a big spider. Some people were really funny about spiders. Now in Nam, those were big spiders.

He spread the newspaper on the dining room table and settled down to check the stock prices. Not that he owned stocks anymore. It was a habit he couldn't break, something from childhood, like making the bed or cleaning the table after dinner. The day seemed off-color without it. *He glimpsed a furry leg before he saw the tarantula.* Later, all he could remember were two intense spider eyes perched on top of two huge fangs.

Description

Explanation

You want your reader to be able to picture the story you have written. Just writing what your characters say and do isn't enough. For example: " 'Don't jump!' yelled John." Is John standing on top of a mountain or in a schoolyard? Is John young or old, skinny or fat, tall or short? Remember that reading is more like listening to the radio than watching television. Readers can't imagine what a scene or a character looks like without help. Use description to show the reader what the setting and the characters look like.

EXAMPLE

A tall, distinguished man in a suit emerged from a battered van and walked toward Tom, smiling. The front end of the van looked like a crumpled bit of paper, painted over with white and brown paint, tinted with rust. Through twenty years of dings, dents, and gouges, no effort had been made to match the bits of various colors of paint in the patches. The inside looked as bashed up as the exterior from hauling lumber, old furniture, tools, wire, cut-up tree limbs, tires, and just about anything else that needed to be hauled. Even now, the back seat had been removed to make room for a burnt-out computer monitor, a large gray toolbox, and an ancient pair of snowshoes. Despite its coat of many colors, the engine turned over with a smooth chup, chup, chup, and the headlamps were new and clean. All the working parts worked well. No showhorse, this was the practical car of a very practical man.

Description often does double duty: It describes and tells the story at once. Though this example is mostly a description of an old van, the reader learns a lot about its owner. The example also creates a puzzle. What sort of a fellow is this man? A practical one, but why is he hauling around a burnt-out computer monitor and a pair of snowshoes?

Tricks of the Trade

- The trick to writing good description is using details. Notice how many details the example (above) uses, all of them small. You don't need to describe everything, however; just use a few telling details that give the reader the idea. Use the activity "Zoom Lens" (Chapter 3, Activity 5) to help you find details.

- Try the background-middleground-foreground method of choosing details: Imagine the scene as a picture. Pick a detail on the horizon, a detail midway between the horizon and the viewer, and a detail close to the viewer.

EXAMPLE

Background	Middleground	Foreground
dust from tractor	elm	shovel and tricycle

The dust from a tractor floated along the horizon, and cicadas sang in the huge elm next to the barn. A battered shovel lay on the lawn next to a shiny new tricycle.

You might reverse the order, describing the shovel, then the elm, and finally the dust from the tractor.

EXAMPLE

A battered shovel lay on the lawn next to a shiny new tricycle. The cicadas sang in the huge elm next to the barn, and dust from a tractor floated along the horizon.

♦ Adjectives add to description, but too many make it dull. Instead of adding adjectives, use less-abstract words. Use an abstraction ladder, which helps writers remember the specific words they know. The top rung of the ladder contains the most general words; each rung below that contains more and more specific words. For the bottom rung, write the specific word you've chosen. Add an adjective, to make it more specific.

EXAMPLES

General	hat
↓	fur hats, straw hats, felt hats, helmets
↓	fedora, panama, boater, bowler, pith helmuts
More specific	a battered panama

General	wire
↓	steel wire, bridge cable
↓	bridge cable, circuit
More specific	a stout bridge cable

Use a thesaurus, synonym-finder, or pictionaries (try Reginald Bregonier and David Fisher's *What's What*) to help you write abstraction ladders.

Dialogue

Explanation

Dialogue is what characters say, as opposed to action, which is what characters do.

EXAMPLE

Alea leaned on her shovel and sighed. *"How much more of this stuff do we have to shovel? My back is aching."*
Jessica laughed. *"Something tells me that your back is in for a bit of a shock. John just left to get another truckload. It takes a lot of manure to grow a garden this size. And it doesn't shovel itself."*
"I don't suppose we could rent an elephant to just hang around in the garden for the spring."

"Oh all right." Laughing, Jessica took the shovel from Alea's hand and leaned it up against the wall next to hers. *"We'll have a cup of tea and a stretch. You can check the phone directory for elephant rentals."*

Dialogue sounds as if real people were talking, but it is not written exactly as people talk. That would be dull, as in the following example, which is all dialogue.

EXAMPLE

"Hi," said Jane.
"Hi," answered Sue.
"Where are you going?" asked Jane.
"English class," answered Sue.
"Me too," said Jane
"I'm not ready for the test."
"Really?"
"I have to go to my locker first."
"Why?"
"To get my notes."

In dialogue, the conversation is compressed, For example, cut "Hi," "Me, too," "Really?" and so forth. We all say these things in real conversation, but they aren't necessary for the reader to understand the dialogue, and they are dull. Once the dialogue is compressed, it is laced with action to show what the characters are doing.

EXAMPLE

(Dialogue is italic; the rest is action.)

Jane caught up with Sue in the hallway. *"Hi. Where are you off to in such a hurry?"*
"English class," groaned Sue. She paused at the intersection of two hallways and shuffled through her notebook, frowning. *"I'm not ready for the test. Better get my notes from my locker."*
"You'll be late," warned Jane, heading for room D3.
" 'Tis far, far better to be late than to flunk."

Tricks of the Trade

♦ Pay attention to making your dialogue sound like your characters. A cab driver in New York and a cowboy in Arizona do not speak the same way.

♦ Make sure your reader knows who is speaking. When you write dialogue, begin a new paragraph each time a different character speaks. Be sure to write "so-and-so said" if it isn't clear from the paragraphing who is speaking.

♦ Instead of using the word *said*, you can use a word that shows action or emotion to indicate who is speaking. (Don't overdo it, though; *said* is best most of the time.) Try using a word or phrase from the following list:

answered	crowed	mumbled	shouted
asserted	declared	murmured	sighed
babbled	demanded	nagged	snickered
badgered	explained	nettled	sniggered
bellowed	exploded	noted	sniped
blathered	fretted	paused	sobbed
blurted	fumed	pestered	speculated
brayed	giggled	pointed out	spouted
bristled	glared	predicted	squalled
cackled	grieved	promised	stewed
chafed	grinned	queried	stopped
chatted	grumbled	raged	stormed
chattered	guessed	rambled on	tittered
cheered	hollered	remarked	wailed
chided	lamented	repeated	whined
chortled	laughed	replied	whispered
chuckled	mimicked	responded	whooped
claimed	moaned	retorted	worried
cried	moped	roared	yelped
croaked	mourned	screamed	

Flashback

Explanation

Writers often don't like to begin at the beginning. They like to begin stories or chapters at a climax. After they have the reader's attention, they use flashback to tell the parts of the story that happened before the climax.

EXAMPLE

Jim Baker swore Dannie would never drag him out for another vacation. He urged the ancient horse along, but it was determined to storm the mountain one aching step at a time.

"Isn't this fun?" laughed Dannie. She guided her elderly mare alongside Jim's horse.

"Great fun for an interior decorator from Manhattan maybe," thought Jim. *He remembered the time his best friend Bob had signed them both up to ride the broncs in the Alamosa Days Rodeo. They were both just kids, but Bob's dad was a rancher and put a high price on horsemanship.*

Tricks of the Trade

Flashback is a useful tool, but getting into and out of a flashback can be a bit tricky:

- Most stories are written in past tense, so the first sentence of the flashback must use the word *had* (*had sighed, had gone, had flown, had begun,* etc.). It's best to use *remembered, recalled, thought back, reminisced about the time,* or something similar to introduce the flashback.

- The easiest way to get out of the flashback and back to the story is to have a character from the present scene say something (such as Danny in the example above: " 'Oh look! A deer!' cried Dannie"). Action also works ("Jim's horse halted abruptly"). Avoid using introspection, description, or narrative to get out of the flashback. They can be used, but it's easy to confuse your reader.

Foreshadowing

Explanation

The word *foreshadowing* means just what it says: "to shadow before." The writer gives the reader a hint—just a shadow—of something to come later in the story. Professional writers use this handy writing tool to solve all sorts of writing problems. Foreshadowing is not hard to do. You can use it, just like a professional would, to make your stories more believable, to plant clues, and to intensify the suspense in your stories.

Foreshadowing for Believability

Everything your characters do or say must be believable to your reader. If a character angers suddenly or easily, the reader won't accept a sudden change of personality to one of sweet patience. Real people don't change that easily or quickly. A character who has little education cannot suddenly know how to use a computer or the principles of particle physics. The reader won't believe it.

Fiction must be believable, at least within the context created by the premises of the story. The premises, of course, may be complete nonsense. Fantasies can have fantastic premises—characters with magic powers, odd places where trees can talk—almost anything the imagination can devise. To be believable, though, the premises must be consistent throughout the story. For example, if the wizard in your fantasy adventure can see through doors in the first scene, your reader will expect the wizard to have the ability to see through doors in all the other scenes, as well. You cannot change the rules of the story on a whim, without explanation.

The need to be consistent can sometimes create problems for story writers. Suppose that the wizard in your fantasy must be able to see through doors, but not through one particularly evil door. You must explain this inconsistency to your reader in a believable way. If you don't foreshadow the event, you will be forced to write a scene explaining why the wizard can't see through all doors just as your characters reach the door the wizard can't see through.

EXAMPLE

> "What's behind the door, Wiz?" asked Beezer.
> The wizard ran his fingers over the roughhewn wood. "I don't know," he said at last. "I have read of a black charm that can close doors even to the eyes of a wizard, but this is the first I have encountered."

There is nothing wrong with this. Your reader has an explanation of the change in the rules. It will be much more believable, though, if you foreshadow the existence of the charmed doors much earlier in the story—perhaps as early as the first time the wizard uses his "doorsight" to rescue your characters from disaster.

EXAMPLE

> "I am sure glad you can see through doors, Wiz," Mr. Beezer sighed with relief. "That dragon would have had us for sure."
> *"Yes, Beezer, but I must warn you. Take care with doors," explained the wizard. "There is a charm, a black charm, that can block doorsight of any wizard. Such doors hide great evil, greater than dragons."*
> "Greater than dragons?" Beezer was alarmed. "How will we know a black-charmed door, then?"
> *"That is my point." The wizard carefully dusted his wand and slid it up his sleeve. "We cannot know. At least, not until it is too late. Take care."*

You can now write your story and lead your characters through a whole series of adventures. When your characters finally reach the evil door, briefly suggest the foreshadowed event and then quickly get to the action.

EXAMPLE

> "What do you see behind this door, Wiz?" asked Beezer grumpily. He was very hungry. Why can't we stop now for breakfast? he wondered.
> The wizard knelt and ran his fingers over the roughhewn wood. "Nothing," he whispered. Then he leaped to his feet and shouted, "Run Beezer! The black charm!"
> Before Beezer could turn, the door exploded in a thousand shattered stars. He shot backwards and bounced from rock to bush down the hillside, finally crashing to a stop at the bottom of a narrow gully.

The foreshadowing helps in several ways. The black-charmed door is more believable to the reader because the reader has been expecting it all along. Better still, the wizard and Beezer are not forced to waste time standing around in front the dangerous door while the wizard explains black charms. The door can explode immediately. Even better, the foreshadowing builds a little suspense into the entire story. Every time the characters encounter a door, the reader wonders, Is this the evil door? (What? You didn't think of having other doors in the story? Get busy and add a couple. Learn to take advantage of these little things.)

Foreshadowing to Plant Clues

Foreshadowing can help you plant believable clues in mysteries. Suppose you are writing a big-city story about Detective Snoop, who is searching for a criminal. One morning, he desperately searches the "mug" books at the station, looking for a photo of the criminal. Later, he happens to pick up a wallet (the clue) on the street, and the wallet just happens to belong to the criminal. Now Snoop knows the crook's name and address. You've planted the clue, but your reader won't believe it because it is so unlikely that Snoop would find just the right wallet on the streets of a big city. However, suppose that at the beginning of the story, a neighbor gives Snoop the wallet to take to the lost-and-found. He throws it in the glove compartment of his car and forgets it. Then, as he searches the mug book much later in the story, he remembers the wallet. That's better, but you may need to do a little more work to make it believable. For example, you might also want to foreshadow the crook haunting Snoop's neighborhood or tailing Snoop himself, so that there is a logical reason the crook might drop the wallet in Snoop's neighborhood.

Foreshadowing to Intensify Suspense

Don't worry about foreshadowing undermining the suspense. On the contrary, suspense builds when your reader expects something but does not know precisely what will happen or when it will happen. For example, as your armies of characters line up for the big battle scene in your story, the reader will know that the battle is coming and that one of the main characters could be hurt. You could heighten the suspense further by foreshadowing the outcome. If you have five main characters, you could write, "When this day ended, only four of the band of friends would journey on." The reader doesn't know who will be lost in battle or exactly what will happen, and keeps turning the pages to find out.

Foreshadowing works best if you blend it carefully, so that it doesn't stick out. One little trick to blending it invisibly is to divert your reader's attention to something else just before you foreshadow an event. In your story about Detective Snoop, he could be in a big hurry just as the neighbor arrives with the wallet.

EXAMPLE

Snoop could not find his car keys. He knew the lieutenant was waiting, and the lieutenant did not like waiting. A lame explanation about lost car keys would draw a withering look and a snooty comment in neat block print on his monthly evaluation: "DISORGANIZED. NEEDS IMPROVEMENT."

Ah, there they were. Snoop fished the keys from under the corner of the sofa, shrugged on his coat, and headed out the door and into the hallway.

"Oh, Bill, I must talk to you . . ."

This was no time for a chat with Mrs. Crabtree. They had been neighbors for years, and Snoop knew from long experience that it was just about impossible to hold a short conversation with his gabby, twinkly-eyed neighbor.

"Can't now, Mrs. C.," Snoop grinned but kept moving. "I'm late for work."

Mrs. Crabtree trailed him down the hallway, holding out a battered, brown wallet. "If you could just take this to the lost-and-found for me, dear. I suppose the police do have a lost-and-found, don't they? I found it on Bond Street on my way to the market. It would take too long for me to turn it in. I don't get around like I used to, you know. My arthritis is awful, and that dratted doctor says there is not much else he can do. I am sure someone must be worrying. It has several credit cards in it. I—"

"Oh, sure, Mrs. C." Snoop circled back, *commandeered the wallet,* and loped off down the hallway, giving Mrs. Crabtree a friendly salute. The lieutenant would be tapping his pencil impatiently right about now. The lieutenant was an impossible boss. *Snoop studied the face smiling at him from the wallet owner's driver's license. Well, he thought as he tossed the wallet in his glove compartment, at least Joseph R. Murphy was going to have a good day finding his wallet.*

Of course, you don't want to hide your foreshadowing too well. Your reader might forget. Before you foreshadow, think of three ways to do it: the subtle hint, the obvious hint, and the stated foreshadowing. You could foreshadow the loss of a character in the battle using any method.

EXAMPLES

Subtle Hint: Gray clouds massed along the hills and the air smelt of death.

Obvious Hint: As Beezer waited for the battle to begin, he watched his companions with some sadness. Would he see them again after this day?

Stated Foreshadowing: Before this day ended, there would only be four to carry on the journey.

Tricks of the Trade

♦ You don't need to know what to foreshadow before you begin writing your story, and it isn't necessary to write your story in order. Just begin writing. If you need to foreshadow an event, find a place earlier in the story to add the foreshadowing.

Introspection

Explanation

Introspection is what your characters think in a scene. There are two ways to write introspection: as internal dialogue or as plain introspection. Internal dialogue presents the character's thoughts just like spoken dialogue using "thought" (or its synonyms such as "remembered" or "imagined") in place of "said" or its synonyms. Unlike internal dialogue, plain introspection does not use "thought" or its synonyms to present a character's thoughts. Plain introspection should be written only where it is obvious to the reader which character is thinking.

EXAMPLES

Internal Dialogue

Allen raced to the bus stop. *Oh no, he thought. I can't be late again. It's my third time. I'll get detention. I don't think Mom's going to understand.*

Introspection

Allen raced to the bus stop. *He couldn't be late again. It was the third time—and that could only mean detention. Mom wasn't going to understand.*

Tricks of the Trade

◆ To avoid confusing your reader, use the point of view of only one character throughout any scene. Don't switch from the thoughts of one character to the thoughts of another.

◆ To move out of introspection and back into the scene, use the flashback reentry technique: Interrupt the character's thoughts with dialogue or action from the scene.

Narrative

Explanation

Narrative *tells* the story, whereas dialogue, action, introspection, and description *show* the story. (In nonfiction—see Chapter 4—narrative tells about the idea, whereas examples, anecdotes, and description show the idea.) Narrative is essential; it moves the story along. It is possible to overdo showing if there isn't much narrative. However, nothing is duller than long paragraphs of narrative, even well-written narrative. Use narrative for a purpose, keep it brief, and practice writing richer narrative.

Beginners often write their first stories entirely in narrative.

EXAMPLES

Then Bill decided to leave India, so he got on a train and went to Nepal. In Kathmandu he met a man in a white suit. Bill thought the man was bad, so he called his boss in America and asked him what to do. Then . . .

Fort Sumter is in Charleston Harbor, South Carolina. It's important because the first shots of the Civil War were fired there in 1861.

There is nothing wrong with a good, simple narrative sentence, but consider making it into a scene. If it's not important enough to become a scene, try enriching the narrative with a little description, action, or dialogue. First write a few simple narrative sentences, but don't use *go* or *went*. Be specific about what happened.

EXAMPLE

Bill got on the train at the Calcutta station. Four days later, he arrived in Nepal. When he got off the train, he was greeted by a man in a white suit.

Next, rewrite the sentences, enriching them with more detail.

EXAMPLE

> When Bill finally climbed the steps to the Calcutta train station, the platform was packed with a thousand people, shouting and pushing. They shoved battered suitcases and curious parcels into one another's backs as they fought to reach seats close to the open windows but far from the locomotive's engines. After a twenty-minute struggle, he finally wedged himself into an aisle seat near the center of the train. Four days later, he stepped off an aged bus onto the streets of Kathmandu. With his first breath of cool mountain air, all thought of steamy, crowded Calcutta slipped away.
>
> "Welcome, Mr. Mendal," said a voice behind him.
>
> Bill turned. The speaker was an odd little man in an impeccable white suit.

You can also enrich nonfiction narrative, although you needn't get carried away. Enrich it with a few more facts, a little description, and perhaps a tiny anecdote.

EXAMPLE

> The city of Charleston, South Carolina, is a city of azaleas and graceful colonial homes. Before the Civil War, its busy harbor was the major Southern port for shipping tobacco and textiles to the wealthy in England and the home of Fort Sumter. Believing that Fort Sumter gave the North a bird's-eye view of one of the South's most precious trade links, Southern Confederates surrounded the Fort on April 2, 1861, and ordered its commander to surrender. When he refused, they fired on the fort, and the Civil War began.

Tricks of the Trade

* Use your encyclopedia and a good atlas to find details. Moving a character from one exotic place to another is a wonderful way to learn about world geography and map reading. Because narrative moves quickly, it requires more research than other parts of the story.

  For the passage about Calcutta above, we used an atlas to discover, for example, that there is no train from Calcutta to Nepal. The train stops at Monghyr, about 200 miles from Kathmandu, the capital of Nepal, and the trip must be finished by bus. Using the map, we measured about 700 miles by train and road from Calcutta to Kathmandu. With delays or irregular bus service, we guessed that the trip might take four days. Kathmandu (population 395,000) is the only place in Nepal large enough to likely have regular bus service. From our desk encyclopedia, we learned that Calcutta is the oldest, most overcrowded city in India (9 million people). It is extremely hot and humid in contrast to Kathmandu, which is in a high mountain valley, with temperatures often below freezing.

  We could have researched further to learn whether the train from Calcutta to Monghyr was diesel or steam, what the passenger cars look like, exactly how long such a trip might take, and so on. Also, we might have tried to discover what the weather would be like in both cities during a certain month of the year.

The need for realistic facts to write the story makes pursuing the facts a pleasure. Conduct a little treasure hunt; use your imagination when researching. It's a fun way to learn. Writing a paragraph about steamy, crowded Calcutta and crisp, cool Kathmandu will make your geography memorable for many years. You may never forget steamy, crowded Calcutta and Kathmandu, high in the mountains.

Research can enrich nonfiction. There are books entirely about Charleston and Fort Sumter, but an encyclopedia and other reference books can help you find the few extra details you need to draw a better picture of graceful Charleston and to depict the opening shot of the war. Use the facts to help you enrich your writing, but don't copy them.

- ◆ Use words such as *told, explained, went,* and *left* in narration to cut out repetitive dialogue or action. (This is the opposite of "Show Don't Tell," so be sure to have a good reason.)

EXAMPLE

Instead of a scene showing Mary and Priscilla discussing the ghost, write:

Mary told Priscilla about the ghost.

Instead of a scene showing Mike walking to the store, write:

Mike went to the store. He wasn't gone long, but when he got home . . .

Transitions

Explanation

To write a story in scenes, the writer constructs several scenes and then hooks them together using transitions. If you have written several scenes for a story, you may be wondering how to hook together the scenes. It sounds easy, but just how do you move your characters from downtown New York City to Washington, D.C. without describing a lot of awkward traveling around while nothing in particular happens? The answer is to write a transition.

A transition is a place in the story where the writer moves the reader from one scene to the next. The most famous transition is a visual one used in silent movies in the 1920s: A card that reads "Meanwhile, back at the ranch . . ." flashes on the screen and then the movie cuts to the new scene at the ranch. This summarizes how to write a transition: First, let the reader know that the place or the time (or both) are going to change; then, begin the new scene. There are 1,001 ways to do this. Two of the best are the break and the stated transition.

First, we need two scenes. Transitions are easier to write if you already know what happens in both scenes. The easiest way to do that is to write the scenes first, then write the transitions. The following example first scene comes from the story about Muskrat and Beaver used in "Weaving Scenes" (Activity 1).

EXAMPLE

First Scene

Muskrat flung a glass into the dish rack. "I will never give another dinner party for the rest of my life," he announced flatly.

"You want everyone and everything to be just perfect," said Beaver. He had enjoyed the party. Muskrat got so fussed up about such minor problems. "Then you get mad and make people uncomfortable when they don't do exactly as you wish."

Beaver opened the kitchen drawer searching for a towel with which to dry the dishes that Muskrat was throwing at the rack. Each drawer was a tidy reflection of its owner. The knives gleamed from careful rows, and the tins of vegetables and fruits were arranged by category. The kitchen towels were folded neatly in the bottom drawer, each embroidered with a saying. Beaver selected "Home Is Where the Heart Is." Perhaps Otter could have been more careful not to spill his grape juice on the carpet. But why have guests if they can't enjoy themselves?

"Mallard put his elbows on the table and was a perfect slob," cried Muskrat. "And the rest of you were behaving like a pack of wild animals."

"Well," answered Beaver, "we are wild animals. What did you expect?"

Muskrat snorted. "That is no excuse for being uncivilized."

Second Scene

Miss Perrybright's School of Etiquette could be found in a shabby building at the far end of a run-down district of small shops. People who are keen to learn etiquette are rarely as keen to pay a high price for it. Nevertheless, two barrels of bright petunias welcomed callers to the school, and an efficient Miss Perrybright personally welcomed them in a spotless front office.

Muskrat liked Miss Perrybright instantly. He knew he had made the right decision as she motioned him to sit in a heavy wood chair opposite her desk.

"I need a good class in etiquette," he blurted out his purpose.

"You must pardon me for saying so, Mr. Muskrat, but your manners seem quite adequate to me," said Miss Perrybright.

Now, use a transition to hook together these two scenes.

The Break

The easiest transition between two scenes is the break. At the end of the first scene, skip a line, type three pound signs (###), then begin the second scene.

EXAMPLE

> "Well," answered Beaver, "we are wild animals. What did you expect?"
> Muskrat snorted. "That is no excuse for being uncivilized."
>
> ###
>
> Miss Perrybright's School of Etiquette could be found in a shabby building at the far end of a run-down district of small shops.

Is that all? Yes, basically. You don't need to explain how Muskrat got from one place to another. The pound signs serve as the transition for skipping to a new scene. Notice, however, that the pound signs tell the reader only that the scene is changing, nothing else. It is wise to reinforce the break to make sure the reader realizes that the story has moved to a new scene.

Remember that scenes take place in one location, during one period of time. Only three things might change from the first scene to the second: a new place, a new time, and new characters. The easiest way to reinforce a break is to mention at least one of these three things in the first sentence following the break ("the school," "the next day," or "Miss Perrybright"). Mentioning the place usually works best.

Of course, some things may stay the same; for example, Muskrat appears in both scenes. Avoid mentioning Muskrat in the first couple of sentences of the second scene. Make sure your reader knows what has changed before you mention something that hasn't changed.

(Incidentally, if you are looking for an example of a break in a published story, pound signs are used only in manuscripts. In published stories, the typesetter uses one or more line spaces to indicate the break.)

The Setup

Another way to reinforce a break is to set up the transition in the first scene. First, write a "setup" sentence mentioning either the new location ("Jenny promised to drive Peter to the *airport*") or the name of one of the new characters who will appear in the next scene ("*Peter* was leaving for Cincinnati that afternoon"). Or, you might mention what time the next scene will take place ("Jenny promised to drive Peter to the airport *that afternoon*").

Read the first scene and find a convenient place to add the setup. You may need to add a little action to the first scene to allow for the setup.

EXAMPLE

> Muskrat snorted. "That is no excuse for being uncivilized."
> Muskrat lay awake for several hours that night, thinking. Finally, he snapped his eyes shut and commanded himself to sleep. *He had made up his mind to visit Miss Perrybright the next day.*
>
> ###
>
> Miss Perrybright's School of Etiquette could be found in a shabby building at the far end of a run-down district of small shops.

Notice how the break is reinforced by repeating the name Miss Perrybright, a new character, in the first sentence following the break. You might use the new place or time in the first sentence following the break ("The *airport* was chaos when they arrived." "*That afternoon*, they caught the plane to Rome.").

Don't be discouraged if it takes several attempts to write a good transition. Transitions take a little patience and practice.

The Stated Transition

Too many breaks give the story a choppy feeling, so you may want to use a stated transition rather than a break. With the break, you don't describe how the characters get from one scene to the next; with the stated transition, you do. Instead of using pound signs, write a simple sentence stating, in effect, "Muskrat went to the city." You can dress this up a bit, of course. Continue the second scene immediately following the stated transition (don't begin a new paragraph). You might need to recast the first sentence of the second scene to allow for the stated transition.

EXAMPLE

> Muskrat snorted. "That is no excuse for being uncivilized."
> *Muskrat woke early the next morning, put on his best suit, and caught the 8:30 a.m. train to the city.* He found Miss Perrybright's School of Etiquette in a shabby building at the far end of a run-down district of small shops.

Reinforce the stated transition the same way you reinforced the break, for example, repeating a key term.

EXAMPLE

> (The key term reinforcing the stated transition is Miss Perrybright. In this example, "the next day" also functions as a setup and reinforcing of the transition.)
> Muskrat snorted. "That is no excuse for being uncivilized."
> Muskrat lay awake for several hours that night, thinking. Finally, he snapped his eyes shut and commanded himself to sleep. *He had made up his mind to visit Miss Perrybright the next day.*
> *Muskrat woke early, put on his best suit, and caught the 8:30 a.m. train to the city.* He found Miss Perrybright's School of Etiquette in a shabby building at the far end of a run-down district of small shops.

If you want to make the stated transition more interesting, expand the transitional sentence into a pint-sized scene by including just a few details of his trip.

EXAMPLE

> He had made up his mind to visit Miss Perrybright the next day.
>
> Muskrat woke early, put on his best suit, and caught the 8:30 a.m. train to the city. The train was packed with animals commuting to work, and Muskrat soon wished he had taken a later train. He forced his way down the crowded aisles, stepping on toes, and receiving sharp looks from his fellow passengers. At last he squeezed his pudgy body into the last seat in the last car. By the time the train reached the city station, his suit was rumpled and he had begun to wonder if this had been such a good idea after all.
>
> He found Miss Perrybright's School of Etiquette in a shabby building at the far end of a run-down district of small shops.

Try writing your own stated transition for these two scenes, first as one or two sentences, then as a mini-scene. Perhaps your Muskrat could drive to town. If you get carried away, you may find that your mini-scene turns into a full-blown scene.

Tricks of the Trade

- Because there are so many ways to write transitions, it helps to collect them and study them. Notice the transitions in the books, stories, and articles you read. Copy into your writing ideas notebook those that seem especially clear and smooth to you. The next time you need to write a transition, use one of your collection as a model.

- Write or rewrite your transitions after you have written the scenes or paragraphs they tie together. Then you can make certain that you have written a transition and check that it is clear.

Editing
with Enthusiasm

An editor should tell the writer his work is better than it is, not a lot better, a little better.

—T. S. Eliot

INTRODUCTION

Editing is an acquired taste, right up there with oysters and fried squid. Students won't undertake it naturally, but with a proper introduction, there is no reason they can't enjoy it. After all, the perfect first draft is an awful burden. It kills creativity with premature judgment and makes drafting harder by mixing the artist and the craftsman. A proper introduction to editing is the key to persuading students to try it. Approach is nine-tenths of the problem.

Some schools using the writing process have labeled editing "getting it right." This may be a poor choice of words. Editing is not simply a matter of correcting errors; it's much more. Creativity is a process of creating something, then adjusting it. These adjustments include changes to meet the writer's creative expectations as well as corrections of mechanical errors. When students revise their work to match their aesthetic sense, they gain a tremendous sense of power. Rather than feeling helpless when they do not succeed on the first attempt, they feel in charge of their writing and more responsible for it. Once they feel in charge, they take more pride in the results. Building confidence and a sense of pride, not "getting it right," are the real reasons for teaching students to edit.

Separating Revision and Polishing

There are two phases to editing: revision and polishing. Students must first learn to separate them and then learn to finish revising before they begin to polish. Mixing revision with polishing invariably creates more work, and many other problems as well.

Revision includes improving clarity, structure, and readability. Students learn to adjust their writing to match their creative expectations when they revise. Revision is also writing-based; that is, students can discuss revisions using writing terminology and can make changes using what they know about planning, drafting, and technique. Revision and drafting are so intimately connected that, for some writers, writing is revision. From the writer's point of view, revision is the most important phase of editing, but it's never a question of "getting it right." There is no correct way to revise a piece, any more than there is only one correct way to write it. Revision is a matter of reworking the piece until the writer feels satisfied.

Polishing includes checking the sentence structure and the finer points of style, improving the punctuation, correcting spelling errors, and (finally) producing attractive copy. Unlike revision, polishing is not writing-based. Each area of polishing is based on an underlying set of skills completely disconnected from the rest of the writing process. For example, a person can know the rules of punctuation backwards and forwards and still write poorly. The reverse is also true. Many talented writers will cheerfully admit that their punctuation is shaky, even though they write well and publish often.

This difference between writing skills and polishing skills is a confusing point, so be very careful about it. Writing is a confidence game. The tentative or uncertain writer always has trouble. Often, students are not confident about their underlying style, spelling, punctuation, and even handwriting skills. If they confuse good spelling, punctuation, or presentation with good writing, they may lose confidence in their writing. Some students conclude that they can't write because they can't spell. Others avoid using any punctuation at all. Still others lose confidence in their ideas and try to conceal them with illegible handwriting. To avoid these problems, teach the skills underlying polishing in separate lessons, separate revision from polishing, and use a light touch with polishing.

Polishing the physical appearance of a piece is the last step to polishing and worth special mention. Polishing the presentation can include anything from making a neat handwritten copy to full-scale desktop publishing. The physical appearance, though, has nothing to do with the quality of the writing. Good penmanship or typing skills may help a student get the words on the page less painfully, but they are not requirements for writing. A messy but well-written story is still well-written.

On the other hand, the world may permit F. Scott Fitzgerald to submit manuscripts scribbled on the back of envelopes but it is less tolerant of the rest of us. An attractive presentation can make the difference between a sale and a rejection slip for a professional writer, and teachers rarely give students full credit for good writing if the presentation is a mess. Because students are always surprised by the amount of time editing consumes, they tend to run out of time and give presentation short shrift. Students should learn to present their work attractively, and they will learn to do a better job if you consistently make sure they finish all the other phases of editing and then give them extra time to work on their presentation.

Selecting Pieces for Editing

Planning and drafting is slow work, but editing is glacial. If students allow twice as much time for editing as drafting, they won't be far off the mark. Because there simply isn't time in the school year for students to thoroughly edit every piece they write, teachers must decide what degree of editing they can reasonably expect.

We prefer to let students choose a few pieces each term to take all the way through the process rather than asking them to do minor editing on every piece of work. Students who choose which pieces to edit have more stake in the results. Each time they thoroughly edit a piece, they learn what it takes to finish a piece of writing.

Recopying a rough draft so that an editor can read it is often the only editing students do; however, these pieces should always be clearly labeled as "neatly recopied rough drafts" or "first drafts" so that students do not confuse partially complete work with finished work.

Distinguishing Editing from Criticism

Before you can persuade students to edit, you must distinguish between editing and criticism. People can be surprisingly cruel about writing. Even sixth- and seventh-grade students may have already received painful criticism of their writing, and they may be leery of the idea of editing because of this experience. The job of the editor and that of the critic only appear to be similar. There is a big difference, a difference too often overlooked.

No sane student—no sane person—shares a rough draft to be shot to pieces. When writers begin to edit, they are still writing and have a long way to go before they finish. They are already exhausted and need encouragement to continue, or they may never finish. Writers do not need criticism at this stage. Those who give it are showing their ignorance.

Writers do need a friendly ear, a fresh pair of eyes, and a different point of view to help them find places that need improvement. They also need a sharp mind to suggest possible changes. Finally, they need a pat on the back to boost their flagging energy. The person who provides all these things is the editor. Good writers love good editors because they are the writer's biggest help and best friends.

Criticism can be devastating to writers. T. S. Eliot moved to England after a heavy bout with some critics and could not write for a year and a half. It damages students to encourage them to throw their hearts into writing something if they are not also protected from the fickle opinions of critics. No writer should judge his or her work on the opinion of one or two people.

We tell our students that once a piece is finished, anybody has a right to comment. These people are the critics. They can say whatever they want for whatever reason. Some critics are serious; some just show off at the expense of the writer; some are thoughtful; some are just silly. Whereas students should listen to suggestions from a good editor, they have every right to ignore a critic. The writer did not ask for the critic's opinion and does not need to listen—even if the critic is a teacher.

Establishing an Editing System

Editing can be complicated and confusing. You must create a simple editing system that is predictable, positive, and based on editing to publish. It doesn't matter what the particular system is as long as it meets these criteria.

Some teachers prefer to serve as editor, but we think the teacher has too much authority to do it well. Teachers' comments, both positive and negative, cut too deep. We prefer a system in which students edit one another's work while the teacher serves as publisher, providing technical assistance and giving final approval. We also integrate the grading system with the editing system to ensure that the two are compatible. (See Teacher's Notebook: On Grading Papers.)

A Simple Editing System

The Editing Process: Break editing into a two-step process: revision and polishing. Break polishing into a series of smaller steps: style, punctuation and spelling, and presentation. Teach students to take one step at a time, and have them seek the approval of the writing group before moving from one step to the next.

The Publishing Payoff: Define a *published work* as "a finished piece that is shared outside the writing group." Publish, in some small way, every piece a student takes all the way through the editing process. For example, display published pieces on an "Authors of the Week" bulletin board or have class readings on a regular basis. Store all published pieces in students' portfolios.

Authors: Authors are responsible for choosing which of their pieces to edit and for making the final decision on every suggestion.

Editors: The writing group is responsible for editing the work of every student in the group. Unless the writing group requests it, the teacher will not read the work until it has been edited by the group several times.

The Publisher: The teacher serves as the "publisher" most of the time. The publisher is responsible for providing technical assistance to the writing groups and for helping students find ways to publish. No piece is published without the publisher's approval.

Grades: Grades are based on writing a certain number of practice pieces, publishing a certain number of pieces, and serving as editor and as copyeditor for at least one other student during the school term. Tell students in advance what they must do to achieve a particular grade.

In this system, the real payoff for writing and careful editing is not a grade, nor is it the opinion of any one person; it is getting published. Students who finish a piece can put it in the portfolios reserved only for published pieces or those ready to publish. They receive special attention for achieving the portfolio and take pride in the accomplishment. At the same time, the teacher can exercise quality control by refusing to allow unfinished or inadequate work in the portfolio. Students work with a predictable set of editors, who must also share their work with the group. The grading system is also predictable. Essentially, students can choose the grade they want to achieve and work toward the goal.

In this chapter we've collected explanations of editing that we think help students get started, together with a series of handouts we use to explain each editing step. In Part 1 are activities that explain editing, define the roles of editors and authors, and introduce students to the *revision loop*, a simple method for identifying what to revise and for generating editorial suggestions. In Part 2 are activities designed to introduce students to the basics of polishing without swamping them in a thousand rules and requirements.

One note of warning: Editing is one of the last great crafts in an age of mass production. Like all crafts, it takes time to develop the necessary skills. Do not automatically expect that students will improve their work through editing. Beginning editors stand a good chance of ruining a draft. When students ruin a piece with their first editorial efforts—and they will—you can try to persuade them to begin again with the original draft, but they may be reluctant, and might even refuse. There is nothing you can do about this. It's part of learning. They will probably do better with the next draft.

PART 1:
INTRODUCING EDITING

The best way to learn to edit is to follow a good example. In the best of all possible worlds, beginning writers would take several manuscripts all the way through the process under the guidance of an experienced editor. So much for pipe dreams. Even if all teachers were skilled editors, one person cannot possibly do editorial justice to a hundred or more students a day. The next best option to one-on-one editing with a seasoned editor is to have students edit one another's work. They do a surprisingly good job if they have clearly defined roles and a clearly defined process. The activities in this part are designed to help students get started: Activity 1 explains editing, Activity 2 defines the roles of editors and authors, and Activity 3 introduces a simple process for revision.

Activity 1:
Editing? What's Editing?

> ∾ Few processes are more wonderful . . . than that of making your manuscript shine where it was rusty, tighten where it was flabby, speak clearly where it mumbled.
>
> —Paul Darcy Boles

We use this little explanation and handout to introduce students to editing.

Instructions to Students

What is editing exactly? Writing a story or an article is a little like creating a garden. The gardener plans the garden by imagining what the garden should look like, deciding where to put the corn and the radishes, and choosing the seeds. Whereas the gardener prepares the soil, plants the seeds, and waters the garden, the writer drafts—but the job doesn't end here. The gardener has weeds to pull, dead plants to remove, and pretty new plants to add before the garden looks its best. So does the writer. There are weedy words to pull, unclear sentences to straighten out, and sections that need to be rearranged—all to make the writing its shining best. That's editing.

There are two steps to editing:

Step 1—Revision: You want to make sure your piece is easy to understand and fun to read. To do this, you revise. When you revise, you can cut words, sentences, or even paragraphs. You can add others. Sometimes, you will need to rearrange sentences and paragraphs; sometimes you will need to rewrite sentences and paragraphs. Revision is always the first step to editing. It's always exciting because you can shape what you have written, to sound just like you want it to sound, without having to worry about deciding what to write, as you did when you drafted the piece.

Step 2—Polishing: Polishing puts the final gloss on your work. When you polish, you check the style, spelling, and punctuation. You also change any little thing that you feel would smooth out the writing. The last step of polishing is typing or neatly recopying the piece so that it looks attractive and is easy to read.

Technically, polishing your presentation is the last step to editing, but really there is one more step—publishing. Why go to all that work if you don't share your story with readers? Any time you share your finished work outside your writing group, you have published it. Publishing is the reason for revising and polishing your stories. You edit because you want to share, to publish. The person in charge of publishing an author's work is called the publisher. The publisher in this class is the teacher. The publisher helps authors and editors solve any problems they can't solve, gives the final approval for publishing, and helps the author find ways to publish.

We're going to tell you more about revision, polishing, production, and publishing as you do them, but in the meantime, we have some rules that apply to all the steps of editing. We call them the Golden Rules of Editing.

The Golden Rules of Editing

<u>Student Handout</u>

Rule 1: When in doubt, read aloud.

The most important part of editing is reading the work aloud to be sure that it sounds just like you want it to sound. If you have a question, read aloud the entire piece, the paragraph, or the sentence. Does it sound right? If it sounds right, it probably is. If it doesn't sound right, it probably isn't.

Rule 2: Take your time.

Editing takes time, but it is time well spent because editing makes your piece the best it can be. If you get tired, take a break. Editing at a steady pace with short breaks always works better than "crash" editing.

Rule 3: Don't mix revision and polishing.

Finish revising before you begin to polish. Mixing revision and polishing always makes a mess. Also, finish one step of the polishing process before you begin the next step. Editing is always easier if you work on one thing at a time.

Rule 4: Always work from big to little.

Begin with big changes, such as moving around entire sections or scenes. Save the little things, such as changing a word in a sentence, for later. It makes no sense to revise a sentence and then cross it out later when you move around an entire section.

Rule 5: Finish.

If you don't finish, how well you write or the care you take to polish won't matter at all. Nobody can read it until it's done. You can take short breaks to refresh your energy, but otherwise, just do the best job you can and keep going until you finish.

Activity 2:
The Editor? Who's That?

〜No passion in the world is equal to the
passion to alter someone else's draft.

—H. G. Wells

Good editors are about as rare as large diamonds; the rest of the world muddles along with a confused idea of the job. Reading rough drafts to strangers is a frightening, unpredictable process. Keep student editing groups together for the entire term. Because students have so few good role models—and so many poor ones—begin with careful explanations of the role of the editor and the proper attitude toward editing.

Instructions to Students

When you edit your work, your attitude is very important. Remember the artist and the craftsman? (See Chapter 3.) Well, the artist is in charge of drafting, but the craftsman is in charge of editing. The artist is enthusiastic, emotionally involved, and sensitive. The craftsman, however, is more like Mr. Spock in the *Star Trek* movies. Mr. Spock is concerned, but he's also detached and logical. While everyone else runs around yelling, Spock stays cool. He listens and comes up with good ideas to solve the problem. He's also patient and takes things one step at a time.

Notice that the attitude of the craftsman is almost the opposite of that of the artist. When editing your work, first tell your artist to take a vacation. Then tell your craftsman to get busy.

The Job of the Editor

You must draft alone, but you don't need to edit alone. You can get help from someone else's craftsman. This outside helper is called an editor. The editor can be a fellow student, a friend, or a teacher.

An editor's job is to give the author a fresh pair of eyes and another viewpoint on the work. A good editor is the author's best friend. When the author is tired, the editor is sympathetic and helps. When the author knows that something doesn't work, the editor suggests what needs to be changed. When the author has made an error, such as a spelling mistake, the editor finds it. When the author can't think of ideas, the editor offers suggestions. If the author's artist overreacts emotionally, the editor gets the author back on track by saying, "Be logical. Cool down." In our class, the members of your writing group will serve as editors for one another.

The author's craftsman and the editor's craftsman work together. On editing days, sometimes you will be an author and sometimes you will be an editor for another student. This works well, as long as authors and editors remember that both are really craftsmen working together. We don't want to be negative, but we must warn you that when either authors or editors do not act like calm, detached craftsmen, the group will have trouble.

When authors act like artists

> they won't listen,
>
> they argue about everything,
>
> they get upset,
>
> they take every comment as a criticism,
>
> they get tired and don't want to finish,
>
> they are impatient.

When editors are poor craftsmen

> they criticize without helping,
>
> they don't take their job seriously,
>
> they make fun of the author or show off at the author's expense,
>
> they aren't specific,
>
> they don't make helpful suggestions.

If the members of your writing group work together as craftsmen, you'll be dynamite. You can help one another, much more than you might realize. We want everyone in our class to learn to be good editors, so we have a handout to remind you of some things good editors should and should not do.

Good Editors

<u>Student Handout</u>

1. Good editors are good craftsmen. They learn as much as they can about writing and apply what they know in a detailed, careful way.

2. Good editors are specific. They don't say, "That's dumb" or "I like that." They say, "Your point needs more suspense" or "The description in this scene paints a good picture of the scenery."

3. Good editors don't boss. It's the author's piece, not the editor's. The good editor makes good suggestions and leaves decisions to the author.

4. Good editors help the author finish. They give the author some pats on the back and say, "Keep going. You're almost finished, and I know you can do it."

5. Good editors help the author take things one step at a time until the piece is finished.

6. Good editors take the job seriously. They feel as proud of the finished piece as the author does—and well they should.

Activity 3:
The Revision Loop

> ～ What is true of friendship is true of editing. . . .
> I have tried to remember that it was my job
> to help when the author needed it, to reassure
> him, to call out of him his best, but always to
> bear in mind that the final decision was his.
>
> —Edward Weeks

For some people, the first draft holds no thrill; only upon revising do they really begin to write. Their motto: "Just give me a telephone directory, anything but a blank page. I'll revise it into something." In every group of students, you will discover that a few catch fire once they discover revision.

"The Revision Loop" provides students with a simple, positive procedure to follow to identify portions of the draft that need revision and to decide how to go about changing them. Before students begin to use the loop, make sure that they feel comfortable with the idea of sharing their work by having them practice reading aloud without comment from other students.

Instructions to Students

Until now, you have been sharing your work with the other people in your writing group. Today, each of you is going to revise your piece with the help of your writing group.

The word *revise* means "to see again." When you draft, you get your story on paper, where you can see it, but no writer finishes in the first draft. It's too hard to think of things to say, write them down, get them organized, and make sure that your work is clear and easy to read, all at once. There are too many things happening. You need to set your piece aside for a while, then take another look. When you see it again, you will find all sorts of things you missed while you were drafting. Some of these things will be good—better than you realized. Other things will need a little more work to make them sound just right.

Revision is the writer's secret weapon. When musicians hit a sour note or downhill skiers take a spill, they can only try to do better the next time. The writer, however, can revise.

A reader may think that a piece was written perfectly the first time, but the writer knows better. Good writers revise and revise and revise until they are satisfied that their work sounds just right. Did you know that Ernest Hemingway revised the end of *A Farewell to Arms* thirty-nine times? Most professionals revise everything at least four or five times. That's why their writing sounds so good.

Of course, you don't need to revise everything thirty-nine times, but you should learn to revise your work until you are satisfied that it sounds right. One of the things that will help you and your editors revise is "The Revision Loop."

(Text continues on p. 171.)

The Revision Loop

<u>Student Handout</u>

1. Group chooses an editorial question

4. The author revises

2. Author reads piece to group

3. Editors make editorial suggestions

The Revision Loop

Step 1: The group begins the loop by choosing an editorial question.

Editorial questions can be about almost anything: "What is the best part?" "How can the author make the dialogue better fit the characters?" "Which sections are not clear?" "How can the author make the end more satisfying?" "How can the author add suspense?" (See the "Basic Editorial Questions" handout for sample questions to ask.)

Choosing those editorial questions that will most help the author is the trick to revising. You can go around the loop as many times as desired, but there are a thousand possible editorial questions. Editors and authors should go around the loop for at least the three or four questions that they think will most help the author.

Choose any question for a loop, but always use "What is the best part?" for the first loop. Strangely, authors do not always know which parts of their stories are best. If their editors forget to mention which parts are best, the authors may accidentally cut them when they revise.

Step 2: The author reads the piece aloud while the editors listen carefully, keeping the editorial question in mind.

Reading aloud is the most important part of editing. *Revision* may be a misleading word because authors and editors do not necessarily need to see a piece, but they do need to hear it. (Remember, writing is like singing. Until a piece is read aloud, it is like an unsung song.) While the author reads, the editors should listen carefully, keeping the editorial question in mind, and take notes.

The first time the author reads a draft aloud, little problems called klunkers become apparent. A klunker is not a big problem. It's just a place where the writer's imagination was moving faster than the pen. The result is missing words or scrambled sentences. Everybody—including the author—says "Huh?" Fix the klunkers at once, to get them out of the way. (If the group can't decide whether or not something is a klunker, it is not. Klunkers are obvious.)

Step 3: The editors make suggestions.

When you are an editor, remember that you think before offering a suggestion. When you do make a suggestion, be specific. Give the author your best ideas, then let the author decide what to do.

Suppose the editors decide to tell the author that the climax needs more suspense. Instead of saying, "Make the climax more suspenseful," say, for example, "I think your climax needs more suspense. Remember that paragraph just before the train comes out of the tunnel—the paragraph about the dog walking along the train tracks? Maybe you could stretch that out just a little more and make us worry a little more about what will happen when the train comes out of the tunnel."

Step 4: The author considers the editors' suggestions, decides what to do, and makes the revisions.

The last step of the loop is for the author to make changes to the piece. The group can wait for the author to make the changes before beginning a new loop, with another editorial question, or the group can do several loops before the author revises.

Try following a few rules when revising your work: Always work from big to little. Work on entire sections first, paragraphs next, then sentences, and finally individual words. When you revise, you can cut, rearrange, add, or rewrite, in the following order:

Cut: Cut unnecessary sections, paragraphs, sentences, or words to remove everything that conceals the good parts of your story, just like a gardener pulling weeds and trimming away dead branches to reveal the pretty flowers. Once you have pulled the weeds, you can better see your story.

Rearrange: Rearrange the order of the paragraphs into a clearer design. Use scissors and tape to cut apart the draft and rearrange the order.

Add: Add any improvements you think will help your newly arranged draft.

Rewrite: Rewrite to improve sentences and paragraphs.

Basic Editorial Questions

<u>Student Handout</u>

To help editors think of specific suggestions, this list includes follow-up questions for each general question.

Nonfiction

1. What is the best part? Why?

2. Does the piece suit the ideal reader? Is the information appropriate to that ideal reader? Is there anything missing that the ideal reader would probably like to know?

3. How does the mood add to the piece? Does the author maintain the same mood throughout the piece? Are there any sections where the mood is inconsistent?

4. Does the author say what he or she wants to say? What is the key idea? Does that key idea come across clearly?

5. What is the most interesting information in the piece? How is it presented? Is it presented in the right place?

6. Does the writer use examples or anecdotes? Do they make the piece more fun to read? Could the piece use more examples or another anecdote?

7. Where is the piece easiest to understand? Are there any places the piece is hard to understand? Why? What could the author do to make it clearer?

8. Are there any unnecessary parts in the piece? Why aren't they necessary? Could the author cut them? How would cutting them improve the piece?

9. Choose two of the following words to describe the piece and explain why you chose them:

clear	entertaining	informative	relaxed
compact	flowing	musical	serious
crisp	funny	organized	sparkling
detailed	helpful	original	well-researched

10. If you were to suggest just one change that the author should make, what would that change be? Why?

Fiction

1. What is the best part? Why?

2. Is it easy to imagine the characters? What makes each important character interesting? Are the things they do consistent with their personalities? Does the dialogue fit the characters?

3. Who is the most interesting character? Why?

4. What is the best scene? Why?

5. Is the story easy to follow? Is there anything that does not make sense? Why?

6. Is the story even? Were some scenes too short or too long? What could the author do to make the story even?

7. Is the ending satisfying? Does the author tie up all the loose ends, or do you wonder, for example, what happened to some characters or how a mystery was solved? What could the author do to tie up loose ends or make the ending more satisfying?

8. Where in the story is the best action, description, dialogue, or introspection? Are there any places where the story could use more of these techniques?

9. Are there any unnecessary scenes, characters, or other parts of the story? Why aren't they necessary? How would cutting them improve the story?

10. Does the crisis have enough suspense to hold the reader's attention? If not, what could the author do to add a little more suspense?

11. Choose two of the following words to describe the piece and explain why you chose them:

action-packed	inspiring	relaxed	suspenseful
entertaining	intriguing	serious	thoughtful
flowing	moody	snappy	well-plotted
funny	musical	sparkling	well-researched

12. If you were to suggest just one change that the author should make, what would that change be?

PART 2:
POLISHING TO PUBLISH

Whereas experienced writers may not draw a sharp line between revision and polishing, beginners should. Revision is based on writing. It can be discussed using the same terms and goals as those used for planning and drafting. Polishing, however, encompasses a whole new world. There are several areas of polishing: polishing the style, polishing spelling and punctuation, and polishing the presentation. Each area involves complex decisions and rules. To discuss these decisions and rules, beginners must first learn a whole new vocabulary, such as terminology for the parts of speech.

When students write using all the words they know and the complete range of sentence structures they use in speaking, they inevitably use words they can't yet spell and sentences they can't yet punctuate. If they confuse polishing with revision, they will also tend to confuse good writing with good polishing—and they will be dead wrong. A piece can be perfectly spelled, correctly punctuated, beautifully presented, and horribly written. Or it can be beautifully written and horribly polished.

We try to take a break after revision, so students can replenish their energies and see polishing as a separate project. Also don't ask polishing questions until students have finished revising their work. Avoid mixing polishing questions with revision questions when you comment or grade. Never try to teach new grammar, punctuation, or style rules through writing complete pieces or paragraphs. Students are too tired, and polishing a manuscript is a ludicrously slow way to learn a rule of punctuation or the spelling of a word. Teach mechanics separately. When you do teach mechanics, assign practice sentences, not paragraphs or stories. For example, never give assignments such as "Write a story using the words on your spelling list." Change such an assignment to "Write ten sentences using the ten words on your spelling list."

When students are polishing, keep in mind that part of their problem has nothing to do with their skills at mechanics. Writing takes as much endurance as it does talent or skill. That endurance is developed by writing consistently every day over a long period of time. In this respect, writing is no different than sports that demand physical endurance. When beginners reach the polishing stage, many run out of steam. It isn't that they don't know how to correct the error or that they don't care. They are just too tired to do it. If you want students to do a careful job, break polishing into little stages and give students rest breaks between stages.

Although it is not always possible, we recommend asking students to polish only those pieces that they intend to publish. Polishing takes time and energy. There really isn't any point in doing it if there isn't a reader on the other end. Most students really don't care that much if the teacher finds fault with the polishing. They do care if their ideal reader (Chapter 2, Activity 1) does. Polishing to publish puts the teacher in a better position, where it easier to point out errors without discouraging students. Students are gladly willing to find the errors and fix them when they are preparing to publish a piece of their choosing. Otherwise, they think that polishing is just nitpicking.

This is a good time to introduce students to the reference works that are the tools of the copyeditor's trade. Young students will not be able to use these books without help, but at the very least, they should know that such books exist. Young students assume that adults know all the rules by magic. It's a relief to discover that everybody needs to look them up—even professional copyeditors.

Keep one copy of the each of following books in the classroom and make a point of consulting them when students ask questions:

Spelling Dictionary: Find a small dictionary with spellings only. Try *The New Century VestPocket 50,000 Words.*

Misspeller's Dictionary: This is a dictionary of commonly misspelled words organized by common misspellings. Try *The Misspeller's Dictionary.*

Usage Guide: We like Phyllis Martin's *Word Watcher's Handbook: A Deletionary of the Most Abused and Misused Words.*

Punctuation Guide: We like Margaret Enright Wye's blessedly short *The Complete Guide to Punctuation: A Quick-Reference Deskbook.* We also like Barron's *The Art of Styling Sentences: 20 Patterns for Success* by Marie L. Waddell et al. (although it is a better teaching tool than a reference book).

Style Guide: The most famous is William Strunk and E. B. White's *The Elements of Style,* but there are many other good choices. Gary Provost's delightful *100 Ways to Improve Your Writing* contains an excellent collection of style tips. The most complete style manual available is *The Chicago Manual of Style* from the University of Chicago Press, a fascinating—if overwhelming—tour of the publishing process, from punctuation rules for writers who are preparing manuscripts to printer's typefaces. It should have the subtitle "Everything you ever wanted to know about editing and more." It's worth keeping one copy in every school, so that students know that it exists and teachers have an authoritative guide to consult for tricky questions. Recently, some other presses, such as the *New York Times*, have published their style manuals in paperback. They are perhaps less complete than *The Chicago Manual of Style*, but they are less expensive and less daunting.

The Chicago Manual of Style is worth special mention, however. Full of ideas for the creative teacher who wants to model the writing classroom on the publishing house, it has the most authoritative and intelligent explanation of punctuation and editing rules found anywhere. You can find ideas for a quick writing or editing lesson on days when you run short of activities by opening to almost any page in the book. By the time students leave high school, they should treat *The Chicago Manual of Style* as they would a comfortable old shoe. If you can spare the time, read it yourself, and read it aloud to students. Keep an old copy around the classroom along with a good dictionary. Consult both often. Your students will thank you someday.

Activity 4:
Polishing for Style

> ∽ It is not intentionally mannered writing that adds up to style, or richly poetic paragraphs, or the frank pursuit of novel prose rhythms. The writer's own style emerges when he makes no deliberate attempt to have any style at all.
>
> Lawrence Block

Avoid asking students to follow particular style rules or imitate a style before they have finished drafting. Good style begins with writing simply and naturally in one's own style. The sound of a writer's own style, the natural voice, is as distinct as a singer's natural voice. There is a difference between singing operas in one's own voice and imitating an opera singer. The first may sound rough but honest; the second sounds ridiculous. Writing styles are no different. Students should write in the natural voice. If they want to polish their style, the time to do it is during polishing.

Instructions for Students

Professional writers use some simple little tricks to perk up sentences. You can use them, too. Follow the style tips in the handout, and your writing will really sound great.

(Text continues on p. 177.)

Style Tips

<u>Student Handout</u>

Tip 1: Use the active voice, not the passive, most of the time. (We really do mean most of the time, not all. Too much active voice can jar readers, just as too much passive voice can bore or confuse them.)

EXAMPLES

Passive: The stories *were written by* the students.
Active: The students *wrote* stories.

Passive: The pen *was broken by* Sue.
Active: Sue *broke* the pen.

Passive: The experiment *was done by* the students in Group One.
Active: The students in Group One *did* the experiment.

To find the passive voice, look for "was _____ by" in the sentence. Change it to active by putting the subject of the sentence first.

Tip 2: Replace abstract nouns with more concrete nouns.

EXAMPLES

Abstract: Beautiful *flowers* lined the path.
Specific: *Blue bachelor buttons and purple daisies* lined the path.

Abstract: A *dog* ran along the fence barking at *people*.
Specific: A *German shepherd* ran along the fence barking at *joggers*.

(Don't overdo it. Use your judgment.)

Tip 3: Use simple, specific verbs that say two things at once.

EXAMPLES

General: *She was sitting* in the car.
More Specific: She *waited* in the car.
She *sulked* in the car.
She *slept* in the car.

General: He *went across* the room.
More Specific: He *marched* to the cupboard.
He *slipped* across to the window.
He *danced* across the room.

Tip 4: *As* is a difficult word, especially in fiction. When you have used *as* in the middle of a sentence, try breaking the sentence into two sentences and reversing them.

EXAMPLES

One Sentence: I don't want to do this anymore, thought Sue *as* she tied another bow on another bouquet.

Two Sentences, Reversed: Sue tied another bow on another bouquet. I don't want to do this anymore, she thought.

One Sentence: Jo wondered what the weather would be like when she got off the plane tomorrow *as* the thunder cracked outside and the first drops of the storm rattled on the window.

Two Sentences, Reversed: The thunder cracked outside and the first drops of the storm rattled on the window. Jo wondered what the weather would be like when she got off the plane tomorrow.

Tip 5: Once is enough. If you've said something twice, cut the weaker phrase.

EXAMPLES

Twice: John walked across the kitchen and yanked open the refrigerator door. As he opened the refrigerator, a mouse ran out from under it.

Once: John walked across the kitchen and yanked open the refrigerator door. A mouse ran out from under it.

Twice: Hannibal led his men across the Alps and onto the plains of northern Italy. As they crossed the Alps, they fought snow and blinding hail and talked of victory once they reached the warm plains.

Once: As Hannibal's men crossed the Alps, they fought snow and blinding hail and talked of a victory ahead on the warm plains of northern Italy.

Tip 6: Replace long, dull words with short, punchy words.

EXAMPLE

Long, Dull: He *demonstrated his happiness*.

Short, Punchy: He *smiled*.

Tip 7: Cut unnecessary adverbs. Look for words ending with *ly*. Ask yourself if you need the word. If not, cut it.

EXAMPLES

> **With Adverb:** She shouted *loudly*.
>
> **Verb Alone:** She shouted.
>
>
> **With Adverb:** It was *totally* awesome.
>
> **Verb Alone:** It was awesome.

Tip 8: Cut useless clutter words, if possible.

EXAMPLES

a little	rather
kind of	really
mostly	sort of
pretty much	too
quite	very

Tip 9—The Big Rule: Read every sentence out loud. Does it say something? Does it make sense? Does it sound clear and simple? Does it fit the mood of the writing? If not, rewrite it.

Style Tips That Don't Work

Bad Tip 1: Put commas where you take a breath.

> Singers spend years learning where and how to breathe. So do writers. Expert writers, who know all the rules of punctuation and proper breathing, can use this rule. If you try it without knowing the rules, you might want to sprinkle commas everywhere, making your writing sound like you have a bad cold. Learn the rules of punctuation and use as few commas as possible.

Bad Tip 2: Don't repeat words.

> This is nonsense. Good writers repeat words all the time. If you change every repeated word to another, you'll sound like a sportscaster. By all means, don't pound your reader to death repeating words. But do use a little repetition for rhythm, emphasis, or reinforcing transitions.

Activity 5:
Polishing for Pride

> Word carpentry is like any other kind of carpentry. You must join your sentences smoothly.
>
> —Anatole France

Like all writers, students, suffer from manuscript blindness. Once a writer has reread a manuscript a certain number of times, even obvious errors become invisible.[1]

Set up a clear process. Include a procedure for checking the spelling and a list of punctuation rules to check. This type of detailed polishing can continue forever, so it sometimes helps to set a time limit. Emphasize copyediting as much or as little as you wish, but don't overdo it. It's better to save the time for separate spelling and punctuation lessons than to waste it churning through manuscripts trying to find errors.

Instructions to Students

You have finished polishing the style in your work. Now we come to the next phase of polishing: copyediting. For school, think of copyediting as checking the spelling and punctuation. In publishing houses, copyediting also includes style questions, fact checking, and other things.

Look at it this way: Leaving spelling errors or sloppy punctuation in your work is like writing a play, then sitting in the audience playing a kazoo while people are trying to watch it. Everybody will forget the play for the kazoo. The same thing happens with stories. Everybody forgets the story and notices the misspelled word. If you want people to notice all your hard work, you must copyedit.

We're going to let you in on a big secret: It's very hard for authors to copyedit their work. There are two reasons for this. First, no one knows how to spell all 600,000+ words in the English language, and no one can remember all the rules of punctuation. The author who does not know how to spell a particular word often won't realize that it is misspelled until someone else points it out. Second, the author often has a little problem called manuscript blindness. Your brain is a fantastic thing. It remembers what you meant to write down, even if you did not actually write it down that way. As you reread your story, your brain fills in the missing words or rearranges the letters, and you don't even notice. After working so long, the author sometimes cannot see the simplest error.

---

1. Teachers suffer from a special version of manuscript blindness. They see so many misspellings and punctuation errors in students' work that their spelling and punctuation deteriorates. The worst copyeditor in the world might be a language arts teacher in the month of May.

What do you think is the secret to polishing? *Find someone to help you.* Two heads are better than one. It does not matter that you know how to spell everything or all the rules of punctuation. It does matter that you care enough to get help. In publishing houses, special editors, called copyeditors, help writers polish these details. In our class, your writing groups will serve as copyeditors.

Today, you will copyedit your stories. Check the spelling first, then the punctuation. We have written on the chalkboard the rules of punctuation that we want you to check. (Note to teachers: Choose whichever rules you are stressing.) If you have any questions, make an appointment to ask a teacher.

We have two handouts to help you. The first handout shows you the steps for checking the spelling. The second handout, "The Personality of Punctuation," is just for fun. It should give you an idea of what punctuation problems to look for, beyond the problems written on the chalkboard.

(Text continues on p. 184.)

How to Check Spelling

<u>Student Handout</u>

Step 1: Mark the words.

The author gives their story to a copyeditor. First, the copyeditor reads through the piece and marks every word with questionable spelling. Don't correct the spelling; just mark it. (Use a bright-colored pen or a highlighter marker. Blue or black marks are too hard to see.) Then the copyeditor gives the piece to another person, either the author or another copyeditor. This second person reads through the piece and marks every questionable spelling that the first person may have missed. Once the piece has been marked twice, return it to the author.

Step 2: Make a list.

The author makes a list on a separate sheet of paper of all the marked words.

Step 3: Check the list.

Using a regular dictionary, a spelling dictionary, or a misspeller's dictionary, the author looks up every word on the list and writes down the correct spelling next to the original spelling.

Step 4: Correct the spelling.

The author looks at every marked word in the piece, crosses it out, and writes the correct spelling above the misspelled word.

Step 5: List your "Dirty Dozen."

Choose twelve words from the list of words misspelled in your piece. These twelve words are your Dirty Dozen. Write down the correct spellings on a separate sheet of paper and save this list. Practice spelling your Dirty Dozen, and keep the list at hand when you write, so you can quickly check the words that give you the most trouble.

From *Teaching Writing in Middle School*. © 1998 Beth Means and Lindy Lindner. Teacher Ideas Press. (800) 237-6124.

The Personality of Punctuation

<u>Polishing Handout 2</u>

punctuation is not something that you must use because somebody made up some dumb rules and said you gotta use them punctuation is part of your writing it helps your reader understand what you are saying when you speak you punctuate by pausing or by changing the way you say something but you cant do this when you write the only way to make your reader understand is to use punctuation stories without punctuation are very hard to read as you can see

Instead of thinking of punctuation as rules, try thinking of each punctuation mark as a person who helps your reader understand your writing.

Good Old Joe, the Period

When do you need Joe, the period? At the end of a sentence. Listen to your sentences as you read aloud. When you reach the end of a sentence (you can hear it), add the period. Begin the next sentence with a capital letter. Good old Joe is always around. He is relaxed, and he keeps your reader from feeling frantic, breathless, confused, and strung out.

Jeeves, the Comma

Jeeves, the comma, is an excellent butler—the kind you miss when he isn't there but hardly notice when he is. He performs many duties. He puts a little pause in the sentence to separate words, phrases, or clauses. In fact, Jeeves is so quiet, yet so busy, that it takes quite awhile to learn when to use the comma. Below are some sample sentences to give you some ideas.

EXAMPLES

Punch, the puppet, is famous in England.
"Punch the puppet!" chanted the crowd.

That's a pretty small rabbit.
That's a pretty, small rabbit.

Whatever happens, happens because of you.

John, who is interested in jazz, bought concert tickets.

The old house, clearly not used for many years, was the gang's favorite hideout.

Jane and Bob, puffing and groaning, finally reached the top of the hill.

Why, Lindy, did you mail the letter without a stamp?
Why Lindy! What a surprise to see you.

They bought baseball bats, balls, and uniforms.

That quilt is black, white, and green.

Did you bring soda pop, potato chips, or hot dogs?

All we ever do is punctuate, punctuate, punctuate!

The dog howled, and the cat meowed.
The dog howled, the cat meowed, and the mouse squeaked.
After the dog howled, the cat meowed.
If the dog howled, the cat meowed.
Since the dog howled, the cat has meowed, and a mouse squeaked.
Because the dog howled, the cat meowed.
While the dog howled, the cat meowed, and the mouse squeaked.

The Loudmouth Question Mark

The rule is to put a question mark at the end of a question. The truth is that the question mark has a loud, irritating voice. Before you use the question mark, decide how loud you want the question to be. Use a period for soft, quiet questions.

Sally, the Semicolon

Sally is shy, and most people don't get to know her, but Sally is very efficient and helpful—a good friend to writers. Sally can replace ", and" for connecting sentences and also introduce examples.

EXAMPLES

She went to the door, and he went to the window, and the rest of us stayed put.
She went to the door; he went to the window; the rest of us stayed put.

He owned many interesting cars; for example, a 1966 Corvette.

The Kibitzers, the Dashes and Parentheses

When you use a phrase enclosed by dashes or parentheses, picture one of the people in the piece stopping the action, turning to the audience, and explaining something. Dashes are briefer, less of a break than parentheses. You can use commas to pause instead of dashes. Be careful (sometimes these pauses are about as welcome as a backseat driver) with dashes and parentheses. Use them only when you want a break in the action.

EXAMPLES

It was a beautiful day, we all thought, for a softball game.

It was a beautiful day—we all thought—for a softball game.

It was a beautiful day (we all thought) for a softball game.

The Ellipsis, The . . . uh . . . what?

If a character is speaking and falters, you write . . . This is called an ellipsis. It indicates an interruption that confuses the speaker, stuttering, or speech trailing off (or words that you exclude from a quotation).

EXAMPLES

"Billy Jo, I got that goat out of the garage. It . . . "

"What goat?" interrupted Billy Jo. "Why would somebody keep a goat in the garage?"

Marallee put her foot in the stirrup and vaulted onto the horse. Not bad for an amateur, she thought. This is fun. I wonder how long George is going to take to . . . Gosh, this horse is big.

The interrupter can be extremely irritating. Use the ellipses only when you don't mind your reader feeling just a little irritated at the interruption.

The Bomb, the Exclamation Point

If the world just blew up, use the exclamation point. Otherwise, avoid it. Beginners always use too many!!!!!

EXAMPLES

The world blew up!

The world almost blew up.

The world could blow up?

The Drill Sergeant, the Colon

The colon helps you get to the point fast. When you bring in the colon, your reader stands and salutes.

EXAMPLES

There are three colors of shoes on that shelf: purple, green, and pink.

Buy all the school supplies listed below:

pencils

paper with three holes punched in it

a three-ring binder

From *Teaching Writing in Middle School*. © 1998 Beth Means and Lindy Lindner. Teacher Ideas Press. (800) 237-6124.

There is a reason I never use colons: I always forget the rules.

If you are going camping, don't forget the essentials: food, warm clothing, and a good book.

Remember, drill sergeants wear people out, so don't wear out your reader with too many colons. In the following example, the punctuation is correct in all the sentences, but the colon completely stops the action. The exclamation point stops it, too, but not as much. The dash and the comma stop it even less. Use the colon only when you want abrupt halts.

EXAMPLE

Hey you: the one with the purple tennis shoes.

Hey you! The one with the purple tennis shoes.

Hey you—the one with the purple tennis shoes.

Hey you, the one with the purple tennis shoes.

Activity 6:
Presentation Checklist

> ∿I love being a writer. What I can't stand is the paperwork.
>
> —Peter De Vries

Some students have strong production values. They have a good sense of design, they like an attractive presentation, and they care about how the finished piece looks. These students are always tempted to skip editing and to begin retyping and tidying up too soon. To others, the presentation is about as important as a dust bunny under the sofa. Who cares how it looks if it sounds good? For these students, production is a boring, unnecessary chore. They'd much rather be writing. Still, presentation is an important part of writing. It should be the last thing students do, however. Book designers in publishing houses don't begin their work until the copyeditors have finished, with good reason. Presentation takes a great deal of time all by itself. Making changes after something has been typed (or typeset) always triples the effort.

Because recopying and typing take so much time and energy, students sometimes wear out before they finish. Word-processing software, if available, can be a big help at this point. Parents can help with typing, but let them know that you don't object. Offering typing services every so often for special pieces relieves students of some of the burden. Typing teachers are sometimes willing to use student pieces as a class project for the typing class. Asking students to illustrate their pieces provides extra motivation for students who think of writing yet another piece as an oppressive chore. Use the "Presentation Checklist" to help students think through some of their presentation decisions.

Instructions to Students

Congratulations to all of you. You have almost finished writing. Sharing your stories with readers is what writing is all about, but you can't share until you have finished. Readers can't enjoy your stories until the story is neatly recopied or typed. Messy stories are just awful to read. It's like watching a broken television: The picture always gets fuzzy at the best part. The last step of editing is presentation. It includes anything that you do to make your piece neat, attractive, and easy to read.

Before you begin, you need to consider where your story will be published. If you are submitting stories to teachers or to writing contests, you need to present your story in manuscript form. Manuscripts are plain. They are neatly handwritten, printed, or typed. They are double-spaced and printed on one side of the page.

The other form of presentation is the galley. Use galleys when your piece will be displayed just as you produce it. The galley can be set up any way you think would be attractive. You can illustrate it with drawings; use different typefaces for titles, headings, and text; and print on both sides of the page to make a booklet. You can single-space, mix typed sections with handwritten sections, and anything else you think would show your work at its best.

Whether you plan a manuscript or a galley, presentation is a lot of work. It's best to think through your decisions before you begin. The "Presentation Checklist" will help you make some of your decisions. We've left space at the bottom of the checklist for you to make additional notes.

When you retype or recopy, you may make an error. Professional writers call them typos, and they hate them because typos are so hard to spot. Always ask one of your editors to read your final copy and mark typos lightly with a pencil, so that you can fix them.

Finally, imagine what might happen if someone reading your story dropped it. Would they be able to put the pages back together in order? Get into the habit of numbering every page. If the person to whom you will give your piece handles many stories (for instance, a teacher or a magazine editor), put your last name and the title on every page.

Presentation Checklist

<u>Student Handout</u>
(Check the appropriate boxes.)

My piece:

1. Will be produced as a   ☐ manuscript.
                                     ☐ galley.

2. Will be neatly handwritten in ☐ longhand.
                                     ☐ print.

   or Typed using a   ☐ typewriter.
                                     ☐ word processor.

3. Will be written or typed on   ☐ one side of the page.
                                     ☐ both sides of the page (galley only).

   and Will be   ☐ double-spaced.
                                     ☐ single-spaced (galley only).

4. Will have each paragraph   ☐ on a new line and indented five spaces.
                                     ☐ two lines down without indent.

5. ☐ Will include illustrations (galley only).

6. Will be titled using   ☐ all capital letters.
                                     ☐ mixed capital and small letters.

   and The title will be   ☐ centered.
                                     ☐ flush left.

7. Will include the page number on each page at the bottom
                                   ☐ in the center.
                                   ☐ flush right.

8. Will include my full name, written or typed
                                   ☐ on the title page.
                                   ☐ at the top of page 1.

9. ☐ Will include my last name, written or typed, at the bottom left-hand corner of every page.

Activity 7:
The Publishing Game

> ✺ For several days after my first book was published I carried it about in my pocket, and took surreptitious peeps at it to make sure the ink had not faded.
>
> —James M. Barrie

Students enjoy models of the real world, and because writing is a lifetime activity, teachers should connect students to the writing world outside. Use this activity after a field trip to a publisher or newspaper or a visit from an author to the school.

Instructions to Students

For the next three weeks you will become part of a magazine publishing firm. This firm needs help getting reestablished. It has been losing subscriptions and is at a loss as to what to do.

As members of the magazine staff, you will form teams of six to eight people. After the next three weeks each team will present the class with a magazine that you think will bring the firm out of this slump.

I. Team Staff Members

Each team will elect the following staff members for the publication:

writers	art editor
poets	format editor
biography editor	promotion editor

(See below for job descriptions.)

II. Theme

As a team, discuss the idea of a theme for your magazine; for example: news, fashion, holidays, sports, hobbies, special audiences, science or technical. After you have chosen your theme, do the following:

1. Design the cover and choose a title.

2. Laminate your cover.

III. Format

Decide on the format for the order of stories and articles that will be in your magazine. The following items should be included in your magazine:

1. cover (design a front and a back)

2. title

3. copyright page (contains facts of publication, name of publishing firm, publication date, and date to appear on newsstand)

4. pagination

5. table of contents (list all titles of articles, stories, and poems)

IV. Contents

Make a list of the types of articles, stories, and advertisements the magazine will contain. Each magazine should have ten to twelve pieces. There can be more than one piece of the same type, but you should include a variety of types. A few suggestions:

book reviews	movie reviews
cartoons	national interest articles
commercial advertisements	poetry
contributor's page	short stories
how-to articles	sports articles
international interest articles	syndicated column

V. Organization

The team will assign pieces to the writers and choose a deadline for submitting polished drafts. As each piece of writing is finished, the format editor should review it. It should be proofread for any errors in form, punctuation, spelling, and grammar. The format editor gives publishing approval.

As soon as the material has been approved for publishing, the writers should recopy the pieces in pen or type them; the art editor should compile and complete the artwork; and the team should compile and construct the magazine. All the materials needed for construction will be available on a table at the front of the classroom. (Note to Teachers: You can get as carried away with production as you wish, but simple materials work just fine. Heavy colored paper works for the covers. Drawings done in colored pencils or markers, gluing colored strips of paper or collage material, and designs in glitter glue can be used for decorating the covers and illustrating the contents. A three-hole punch with string or heavy staples can be used for binding.)

VI. Promotion

Once the magazine is ready, the promotion editor will prepare a promotion idea and present the team's magazine to the class for sale.

Job Description: Writer

Writers are responsible for the written portion of the magazine. Writers can ask members of the team to help them with revision editing, but the format editor does the final copyediting. Each writer may be assigned to write any number of articles, some of which the team may decide not to use. Writers can use pieces from their portfolio folder. They should also choose pictures or draw illustrations of their stories to make them more interesting. Writers may want to read magazine articles for ideas and to find examples of styles for stories.

Job Description: Biography Editor

The biography editor interviews the writers, poets, and editors in your team about their hometowns, main interests, previous publications, and personal lives. The biography editor uses this information to write a forty- to fifty-word "Contributor's Note" (a biography) for each member of the team. (Note: Writers can make up their backgrounds.)

EXAMPLE

John Doe is a contributing editor to (*name of magazine*) . His stories have appeared in *Mud* magazine and in *Scholastick Scope.* His latest venture is the founding of a new journal about the popular arts, *The Coyote Review.* John is a bachelor and lives in Yuma, Arizona, with his pet beagle, Lucky.

Job Description: Art Editor

The art editor is in charge of all the pictures and artwork in the magazine. He or she places the art on the page and does any necessary lettering. The art editor can cut and paste artwork from the magazines contributed by the team, use computer software, or draw the artwork. Remember, a neat magazine increases sales.

Job Description: Format Editor

The format editor is the quarterback of the team. He or she decides how the various parts of the magazine will be put together and gives publishing approval to incoming pieces. The format editor should talk to all staff members to learn what articles they are working on and then make a list of the titles and lengths of the articles. The format editor makes sure everyone does their job. Specific jobs of the format editor:

1. Make a table of contents of all articles, poems, and stories for the magazine. Assign page numbers to each piece.

2. Make a copyright page for the magazine following a book or magazine copyright page as an example. Include the facts of publication, the name of your firm, the publication date, and the date the magazine is to appear on the newsstand.

3. Copyedit and proofread every piece. Correct grammar, spelling, and other errors. (Writers who finish early should help with this job.)

Job Description: Promotion Editor

The promotion editor creates a three-minute speech calculated to "sell" the team's magazine to potential buyers, such as students in other classes. Tips:

1. Make the speech as persuasive as possible, explaining why the audience should buy this magazine and what interesting articles it contains. Consider the strong points of the magazine and the kinds of people who may want to buy it—the magazine's ideal readers.

2. Use specific information in your speech, such as

   a. titles and writers for each story, poem, and article,

   b. title and price of the magazine,

   c. biographical information about the writers and editors on the staff (talk with the biography editor).

3. Write a rough draft and practice the speech in front of members of the team.

4. Once the magazine has been assembled, practice delivering the speech to the entire team, with enthusiasm.

5. As an added gimmick, make sample order forms. Mention them in the speech to sell subscriptions.

TEACHER'S NOTEBOOK

On Grading Papers

As every writing teacher knows, grades and writing don't mix. Grades do everything good editors should not. Good editors are specific; grades aren't. Good editors help the writer finish; grades don't. Good editors don't act like critics; grades do. Grades teach students to measure their work against the opinion of just one person—something writers should never do. It is difficult to conceive of a worse editorial system than the traditional system of mark and grade. Still, students, parents, and school administrators expect grades. The trick is to find a grading method that doesn't violate the principles of good editing. Whatever method you use, think it through carefully and try to follow these general principles:

1. Establish clear, written standards in advance.

    Teachers vary greatly in the standards they emphasize. Some stress structure and content while others want every footnote properly formatted. Without clear, written standards, students ping-pong from teacher to teacher guessing from a thousand possibilities what any particular teacher believes important.

    You need not mention whether you stress content, organization, or imagination. We simply list the number of practice pieces and portfolio pieces (see "Teacher's Notebook: On Personal, Practice, and Portfolio Assignments," Chapter 1) a student must complete in a term to receive an A, B, or C. We don't worry too much about the quality of the practice pieces as long as students make a genuine effort. When students turn in work that is not ready for publishing approval, we make a specific list of the things they must do before they will receive approval.

2. Provide students with the opportunity to raise a grade by editing.

    Students do not have much incentive to edit under the traditional method of marking the paper with comments and returning it with a grade. Many don't even read the comments. Why should they? They can't change the grade. Always give students the chance to read the comments and edit accordingly to raise their grade. In our system, students who fall short of the number of pieces needed to achieve the grade they want can always do more practice pieces or edit a piece to portfolio standards.

3. Avoid giving a grade for a paper—either good or bad—without explaining why.

   If students don't know why they received an A instead of a C, or vice versa, they will guess why. Their reasons can range from getting an A because they wrote precisely 284 words to getting a C because they did not use enough commas. These wrong guesses are extremely damaging in the long run. The next time, they will add padding or throw in a thousand extra commas at random in hope of success. Learning to write by this lottery method is neither efficient nor fair.

4. Avoid stressing one set of standards in the assignment and another in the grading.

   Teachers should not stress the content of the writing in the assignment and then mark down for spelling or manuscript preparation alone (although some inexperienced teachers do fall into this trap at first), but it is easy to do it by accident. Marking just the spelling errors and then giving the grade for content can leave a student with a misunderstanding. Do not mark spelling or format errors if the grade stresses content. On a separate "comment" sheet, write something along the lines of "This assignment didn't count spelling, but you need to work on spelling."

5. Grade over several assignments.

   Most professionals throw away perhaps one of every three pieces. It's difficult to make any given piece turn out as desired. Students work under tight deadlines and do not always have the time to try again. Give grades over several assignments and give students the option of throwing out at least one piece with which they are dissatisfied. In our system, students don't need to worry about flops. They can count them as practice pieces and work on the pieces that did turn out as desired.

6. Avoid establishing a fixed percentage of a grade for spelling or presentation.

   Students who have penmanship problems or difficulty spelling cannot correct the problem overnight. If spelling or penmanship counts as a fixed percentage of all writing grades, marking down the work of these students will seem to be something permanent. They soon become discouraged with writing altogether, even though they have the potential to write well.

7. Do your own assignments.

　　If you want students to try a specific genre or technique, to write about a particular subject, or to cover certain major points, first do the assignment yourself. The more detailed the requirements, the more important this is. We have seen countless writing assignments with such conflicting requirements that few people could write such a piece. Science, social studies, and English teachers assigning literary criticism should be especially careful. Take a look at the prewriting choices implied by the assignment and try to write several good openings that would lead into such a piece. If you can't do it, your students probably won't be able to do it either.

8. Avoid marking up final copies.

　　Teachers can't expect students to care about the appearance of their work if their teachers constantly destroy the result by marking all over it. Even seeing "A Good Job!" written on an assignment can be disappointing if it means retyping the first page to have a clean copy. Make a point of writing your comments on a separate sheet of paper. Students appreciate teachers who show respect for their efforts.

On Writing and Spelling

　　Curiously, spelling poses a particular problem for writers. The English language, with its huge vocabulary and flexibility, is one of the most beautiful languages for writing, but its spelling is a mess. In English, the sound of words is not consistently connected with the spelling, nor can any rule be consistently applied. Despite numerous attempts at spelling reform and a thousand efforts to teach this hodgepodge "scientifically," the only way to learn to spell an English word is to memorize how it looks, ignoring for the most part how it sounds.

　　Spelling favors people who remember how words look (visual memory). It penalizes those who remember how they sound (auditory memory). The best spellers are those with good visual memory and poor auditory memory. The next best are those with good visual memory and good auditory memory. Worst of all are those poor souls with a good auditory memory but poor visual memory—they'll be labeled "bad spellers" all their lives.

　　Drafting, by contrast, favors auditory memory. Writing is like singing. Remembering the sound and the flow of words helps writers draft realistic dialogue, write musical description and metaphors, and structure fluent sentences. The result, unfortunately: Those with great natural talent for writing are often poor spellers. Mark Twain is a classic example. He couldn't spell his way off the Mississippi, yet his ear for American English was so acute that he laid the foundation for American literature the day *Huckleberry Finn* was published.

Young students, who are learning to spell as they learn to write, have a dangerous tendency to confuse good spelling with good writing. If they struggle with spelling, they may conclude that they cannot write and give it up. Be especially careful with young students or those with spelling problems to praise the writing before mentioning spelling problems. Avoid mixing comments on the writing with spelling corrections. Never downgrade a piece because of the spelling. Help students correct the spelling and use rough drafts to make lists of the words that give them the most trouble to use later for practice (see Activity 5, Polishing for Pride, for use of the "Dirty Dozen"). Working on troublesome words a few at a time is the easiest way to improve spelling.

On Simple Ways to Publish

Teachers often dread publishing because it can become a time-consuming hassle, but for students, publishing is the fun part. It's disappointing to make such an effort if there is no payoff, so try to keep a list of simple publishing techniques handy. You can save yourself a great deal of effort if you don't try to publish *en masse*. Collect student work in their portfolios and then publish a few students at a time. Here's a list of suggestions:

1. **Day-to-Day Publishing:** Our standard publishing method is to display copies of student work, along with a biography and a picture, on an "Authors of the Week" bulletin board. It's quick and simple. Students enjoy reading the work of students who published that week, and each student who does publish receives a little more attention. Another quick method of publishing is to have students read aloud their work at a "reading" before the class, during a school assembly, or at a lunchtime gathering. Don't forget the morning announcements over the school intercom for poetry and fillers. Finally, the class anthology is always popular with students because they get to be part of a book. Select ten to fifteen students who have pieces ready and ask them to design the cover, draw the illustrations, and create the table of contents. Photocopy the anthology for each student.

2. **Recordings:** Have students record their stories on cassette (complete with sound effects) or videotape. Publish them by lending the cassettes and videotapes to a local nursing home, libraries for the blind and handicapped, or the local children's hospital. Public radio stations are sometimes willing to help students record and broadcast the work, as are the public access divisions of local cable networks.

3. **School Exchanges:** Middle school and high school students enjoy sharing their stories with younger students through readings and recordings. One of our favorite projects is to have students choose a particular elementary or middle school student as an ideal reader, write a story especially for that student, and personally read the story to the ideal reader. School writing clubs might hold joint readings or exchange recordings.

4. **Letters:** Letters are an excellent way to publish because students are likely to receive a response. Politicians are always good about responding, and students enjoy expressing their opinions on subjects of interest. In our experience, students who have written to their favorite authors have often received warm, encouraging letters in return. Many children's authors, especially those who are not famous and swamped with mail, make a point of personally responding to every child who writes.

5. **Contests:** Writing contests are always good places to submit student work, but students should be aware that most contests receive hundreds, if not thousands, of entries. It does not mean they are poor writers if they don't win. It just means that they have a lot of competition. (Be sure students follow the contest rules.)

   The Writer's Market publishes a list of nationwide contests and keeps the list updated in its monthly issues. The best contests, however, are usually local. Check with local civic clubs and citizens groups. Those that don't sponsor a contest already might be persuaded to do so. For example, the Puget Sound Chapter of the L-5 Society, a citizens' group interested in space exploration, was persuaded by one writer to sponsor a contest for students writing about space. The contest was judged by a local science fiction writer, and meeting an astronaut was part of the prize. Keep a list of teachers in your district who are interested in contests. Sometimes a ready-made list of contacts will encourage groups to sponsor a contest. Look in *The Writer's Market* for the names and locations of local writers' conferences. Most communities sponsor a contest every year, and some have categories for student work. Ask the school writing club or the

PTSA to sponsor a contest, if they don't already. The awards do not need to be spectacular: a copy of a book by the winner's favorite author, a certificate, or ribbon will do.

6. **Publishers:** *The Writer's Market* and its companion, *Fiction Writer's Market*, are published by Writer's Digest Books each fall. They list most of the publishers in the country along with what sorts of pieces each publisher wants. These books also have articles about how to write query letters and how to prepare manuscripts, as well as other tips on publishing. They list the names and addresses of agents, writing groups, and organizations that sponsor contests and awards.

In our experience, however, students have about as much chance of publishing through a commercial publisher as they have of being struck by lightning. Publishing houses receive thousands of what they call manuscripts, "over-the-transom" that is, those sent in without a request from the publisher. Most go right back with only a cursory rejection. Some go straight into the wastebasket without a reply. Exceptional student work has a better chance of being published in local magazines, small magazines, education magazines (such as *Scholastic Scope*), and highly specialized magazines. For example, one of our students, whose main aim in life was to be a mechanic, wrote a piece about a day at the drag races. After much pushing to get the piece polished, we sent it to a drag-racing magazine on the off-chance of getting it published. To our surprise, they accepted it. It was quite a thrill to receive recognition from people whose opinion he valued. This is rare, however. Publishing a regular school magazine is just about as much work and may be a better option in the long run.

7. **The Internet:** The Internet has opened up whole new vistas for all kinds of publishing. Check with your faculty Internet advisor to learn more about the possibilities for publishing student work. Visit "Beth's Writing Roundup" site at

> http://www.accessone.com/~beth

for other ideas.

8. **The School Writing Club:** In every school are students who are crazy about writing. They need a writing club, so they can meet others who share their interest. The writing club might sponsor visiting authors, organize readings and contests, publish a magazine, and do other things related to writing. Just the chance to share their stories with other interested students makes this a great opportunity for students. In turn, the writing club heightens the visibility of writing in the entire school. If students are looking for a motto, any of the epigraphs in this book are dandy.

NOTES
FROM THE PROS

On Writing and Publishing
Outside of School

Writing can be a lifetime hobby, and it can become a profession. If you just want to write stories and personal journals for your own entertainment, you need only a notebook and a pen, but why not join the rest of the writing world?

Here's how to start. First, find a writing group. In writing groups, writers read their work to the group and get editing help from the group. Local bookstores, writing magazines, and writers' conferences keep lists of such groups—or just ask some friends who also want to write. Age is not a barrier. Many groups are perfectly happy to have younger writers join them, as long as the writers are enthusiastic about writing. It's much easier to keep writing if you are preparing something to read to a readily available writing group. A lot of writers stay with their group or at least members of it for decades.

The book that professional writers use to find out about the publishing industry is *Writer's Market.* This big book comes out yearly. It lists thousands of publishers of books and magazines. It also lists writer agents, contests, and writing conferences. If you want to know "is there a writers conference near my home," the *Writer's Market* has a list. It has articles all through it on subjects such as preparing your manuscripts for the publisher, writing letters to publishers, and working with editors. Check your school media center. If it doesn't have a copy, your local public library is sure to.

Get to know your library, too. The bulletin board is the best place to check first. Libraries receive lists of writing contests, flyers about visiting authors, and they usually post them on the bulletin board. Tell the reference librarian what you want.

Don't forget the local bookstore. Many of them keep lists of local writing groups, writing contests, and notices of visiting authors. Many sponsor visiting authors to come to the bookstore. Go visit them, especially those that do the type of writing you enjoy most. Ask them how they got started, or ask for advice on how to write and publish in their field.

Study them for editorial advice. Some genres, such as science fiction and mystery, hold big conventions. You may be able to attend one. And don't forget writers conferences. These are listed in the *Writer's Digest* and posted on the bulletin boards at local libraries and bookshops.

And of course, keep writing.

∾ Outside of a dog, books are man's best friend. Inside of a dog, it's too dark to read.

—Groucho Marx

Bibliography

Adelman, Robert H. *What's Really Involved in Writing and Selling Your Book.* Los Angeles: Nash, 1972.

Asimov, Isaac. *Isaac Asimov's Book of Facts.* Arenal, NJ: Random House, 1991.

———. *Fantastic Voyage.* Boston: Houghton Mifflin, 1966.

———. *I, Robot.* New York: Ballantine Books, 1983.

Baker, Samm Sinclair. *Writing Nonfiction That Sells.* Cincinnati, OH: Writer's Digest Books, 1986.

Bartlett, John. *Familiar Quotations.* Secaucus, NJ: Citadel Press, 1983.

Bates, Jefferson D. *Writing with Precision: How to Write So That You Cannot Possibly Be Misunderstood.* Washington, DC: Acropolis Books, 1983.

Bethancourt, T. Ernesto. *Dog Days of Arthur Cane.* New York: Holiday House, 1976.

Block, Lawrence. *Writing the Novel from Plot to Print (A Step-by-Step Guide from Idea to the Final Sale).* Cincinnati, OH: Writer's Digest Books, 1986.

Bocca, Geoffrey. *You Can Write a Novel.* Englewood Cliffs, NJ: Prentice-Hall, 1983.

Boeschen, John. *Freelance Writing for Profit: A Guide to Writing and Selling Nonfiction Articles.* New York: St. Martin's Press, 1982.

Boggess, Louise. *Article Techniques That Sell.* San Mateo, CA: B & B Press, 1978.

Boles, Paul Darcy. *Storycrafting.* Cincinnati, OH: Writer's Digest Books, 1984.

Bradbury, Ray. *The Veldt.* Mankato, MN: Creative Education, 1987.

Brande, Dorothea. *Becoming a Writer.* Los Angeles: J. P. Tarcher, 1981.

Bregonier, Reginald, and David Fisher. *What's What: A Visual Glossary of the Physical World.* New York: Ballantine Books, 1982.

Buzan, Tony. *Use Both Sides of Your Brain.* New York: E. P. Dutton, 1983.

Carroll, Lewis. *Alice in Wonderland.* New York: Putnam, 1986.

Charlton, James, ed. *The Writer's Quotation Book: A Literary Companion.* New York: Penguin Books, 1981.

Cheney, Theodore A. *Getting the Words Right: How to Revise, Edit & Rewrite.* Cincinnati, OH: Writer's Digest Books, 1984.

The Chicago Manual of Style: For Authors, Editors, and Copywriters. 14th ed. Chicago: University of Chicago Press, 1993.

Collins, Wilkie. *The Moonstone.* New York: Paperback Library, 1966.

Consumer Reports. Yonkers, NY: Consumers Union, 1936- . (Periodical).

Cook, Claire Kehrwald. *The MLA's Line by Line: How to Edit Your Own Writing.* Boston: Modern Language Association of America; Boston: Houghton Mifflin, 1985.

Cross, Peter R., ed. *Write a Teacher-Aid Book.* Belmont, CA: Fearon-Pitman, 1978.

Daniels, Harvey A. *Famous Last Words: The American Language Crisis Reconsidered.* Carbondale and Edwardsville: Southern Illinois University Press, 1983.

De Montaigne, Michel. *Montaigne Essays.* New York: Viking Penguin, 1993.

Dean, John F. *Writing Well: 60 Simply-Super Lessons to Motivate and Improve Students' Writing.* Belmont, CA: David S. Lake, 1985.

Delton, Judy. *The Twenty-Nine Most Common Writing Mistakes and How to Avoid Them.* Cincinnati, OH: Writer's Digest Books, 1985.

Doyle, Sir Arthur Conan. *The Complete Sherlock Holmes.* 2 volumes. Garden City, NY: Doubleday and Company, 1930.

Doyle, Michael, and David Straus. *How to Make Meetings Work: The New Interactive Method.* New York: Berkley, 1976.

Edwards, Betty. *Drawing on the Right Side of the Brain: A Course in Enhancing Creativity and Artistic Confidence.* Los Angeles: J. P. Tarcher, 1979.

Edwards, Charlotte. *Writing from the Inside Out.* Cincinnati, OH: Writer's Digest Books, 1984.

Elbow, Peter. *Writing with Power: Techniques for Mastering the Writing Process.* New York: Oxford University Press, 1981.

Ephron, Delia. *How to Eat Like a Child, and Other Lessons in Not Being a Grown-Up.* New York: Viking Penguin, 1978.

Evans, Bergen. *Dictionary of Quotations.* New York: Delacorte Press, 1968.

Fader, Daniel. *The New Hooked on Books: How to Learn and How to Teach Reading and Writing with Pleasure.* New York: Berkley, 1982.

Francis, Dick. *Flying Finish.* New York: Pocket Books, 1975.

————. *The Racing Game (Odds Against).* New York: Pocket Books, 1984.

————. *Reflex.* New York: Fawcett Crest, 1982.

Goldberg, Natalie. *Writing Down the Bones: Freeing the Writer Within.* Boston: Shambhala, 1986.

Grahame, Kenneth. *The Wind in the Willows.* New York: Charles Scribner's Sons, 1960.

Graves, Donald H. *Writing: Teachers and Children at Work.* Portsmouth, NH: Heinemann Educational Books, 1983.

Griffith, Benjamin W. *A Pocket Guide to Literature and Language Terms.* Woodbury, NY: Barron's Educational Series, 1986.

Henry, O. *The Ransom of Red Chief.* Mankato, MN: Creative Education, 1980.

Herriot, James. *All Creatures Great and Small.* New York: St. Martin's Press, 1972.

———. *James Herriot's Dog Stories.* New York: St. Martin's Press, 1986.

Holm, Kristen C., ed. *Writer's Market, 1998: Where and How to Sell What You Write.* Cincinnati, OH: Writer's Digest Books, 1997.

Holt, John. *Freedom and Beyond.* New York: Dell, 1973.

———. *The Underachieving School.* New York: Dell, 1970.

Hudson, Kenneth. *The Dictionary of Even More Diseased English.* Chicago: Academy Chicago, 1983.

Kane, Eileen. *Doing Your Own Research: How to Do Basic Descriptive Research in the Social Sciences and Humanities.* London: Marion Boyars, 1985.

Kendall, Carol. *The Gammage Cup.* San Diego, CA: Harcourt Brace Jovanovich, 1986.

Kennedy, X. J., and Dorothy M. Kennedy, eds. *The Bedford Reader.* Bedford, TX: Bedford Books, 1984.

Kipling, Rudyard. *Just-So Stories.* New York: Macmillan, 1982.

Klauser, Henriette Anne. *Writing on Both Sides of the Brain: Breakthrough Techniques for People Who Write.* San Francisco: Harper & Row, 1986.

Knapp, Daniel, and John Dennis. *Writing for Real.* Englewood Cliffs, NJ: Prentice-Hall, 1972.

Ladies Home Journal. New York: Meredith, 1883- . (Periodical).

L'Amour, Louis. *Sackett's Land.* Thorndike, ME: Thorndike Press, 1998.

Leavitt, Hart Day, and David A. Sohn. *Look, Think & Write: Using Pictures to Stimulate Thinking and Improve Your Writing.* Lincolnwood, IL: National Textbook, 1986.

LeGuin, Ursula K. *Rocannon's World.* New York: Ace Books, 1980.

Lewis, Norman. *Word Power Made Easy: The Complete Handbook for Building a Superior Vocabulary.* New York: Pocket Books, 1979.

London, Jack. *To Build a Fire.* Mankato, MN: Creative Education, 1980.

Macrorie, Ken. *Twenty Teachers.* New York: Oxford University Press, 1984.

Madsen, Sheila, and Bette Gould. *The Teacher's Book of Lists.* 2d ed. Reading, MA: Addison-Wesley, 1994.

Martin, Harold C. *The Logic & Rhetoric of Exposition.* New York: Rhinehart, 1958.

Martin, Phyllis. *Word Watcher's Handbook: A Deletionary of the Most Abused and Misused Words.* New York: St. Martin's Press, 1982.

McCaffrey, Anne. *The Dragonriders of Pern.* New York: Ballantine Books, 1979.

McGinnis, Alan Loy. *Bringing Out the Best in People: How to Enjoy Helping Others Excel.* Minneapolis, MN: Augsburg, 1985.

McManus, Patrick F. *A Fine and Pleasant Misery*. New York: Holt, Rinehart & Winston, 1978.

———. *Never Sniff a Gift Fish*. New York: Holt, Rinehart & Winston, 1983.

———. *They Shoot Canoes, Don't They?* New York: Holt, Rinehart & Winston, 1981.

Mencken, H. L. *The American Language*. New York: Alfred A. Knopf, 1986.

Merlyn's Pen. East Greenwich, RI: Merlyn's Pen, 1985- . (Periodical).

The Misspeller's Dictionary. New York: Simon & Schuster, 1983.

Morris, William, and Mary Morris. *Morris Dictionary of Word and Phrase Origins*. Vols. 1–3. New York: Harper & Row, 1977.

Murray, Donald M. *A Writer Teaches Writing*. Boston: Houghton Mifflin, 1985.

National Geographic. Washington, DC: National Geographic, 1888- . (Periodical).

The New American Desk Encyclopedia. New York: New American Library, 1984.

Ohuigin, Sean. *Scary Poems for Rotten Kids*. Windsor, Ontario, Canada: Black Moss Press, 1983.

Owen, David. *None of the Above: Behind the Myth of Scholastic Aptitude*. Boston: Houghton Mifflin, 1985.

Pascal, Francine. *Hangin' Out with Cici*. New York: Dell, 1986.

Paterson, Katherine. *Bridge to Terabithia*. New York: Thomas Y. Crowell, 1977.

Paulsen, Gary. *Dogsong*. New York: Bradbury Press, 1985.

———. *Mr. Tuckett*. New York: Funk & Wagnalls, 1969.

Perelman, S. J. *The Best of S. J. Perelman*. New York: Barnes & Noble, 1994.

Peter, Laurence J. *Peter's Quotations: Ideas for Our Time*. New York: Bantam Books, 1980.

Phillips, Kathleen C., and Barbara Steiner. *Creative Writing: A Handbook for Teaching Young People*. Littleton, CO: Libraries Unlimited, 1985.

Polking, Kirk, Joan Bloss, and Colleen Cannon. *Writer's Encyclopedia*. Cincinnati, OH: Writer's Digest Books, 1986.

Popular Science. New York: Popular Science, 1872- . (Periodical).

Provost, Gary. *100 Ways to Improve Your Writing*. New York: New American Library, 1985.

Rico, Gabriele Lusser. *Writing the Natural Way: Using Right-Brain Techniques to Release Your Expressive Powers*. Los Angeles: J. P. Tarcher, 1983.

Rockwell, F. A. *How to Write Plots That Sell*. Chicago: Contemporary Books, 1975.

Rodale, J. I. *The Synonym Finder*. Emmaus, PA: Rodale Press, 1978.

Ross-Larson, Bruce. *Edit Yourself: A Manual for Everyone Who Works with Words*. New York: W. W. Norton, 1985.

Saling, Ann. *The Foundations of Fiction*. Edmonds, WA: Ansal Press, 1984.

Sharp, Harry, ed. *New Century Vest Pocket: 50,000 Words Divided and Spelled*. Rev. ed. Clinton, NJ: New Win, 1978.

Shute, Nevil. *The Far Country.* London: Pan Books, 1967.

Silverstein, Shel. *Where the Sidewalk Ends: Poems & Drawings.* New York: Harper & Row Junior Books, 1974.

Smart, William. *Eight Modern Essayists.* New York: St. Martin's Press, 1965.

Smith, Frank. "Reading Like a Writer." *Language Arts* 60, no. 5 (May 1983): 558–67.

Solzhenitsyn, Aleksandr I. *Gulag Archipelago, 1918–1956: An Experiment in Literary Investigation.* New York: Harper & Row, 1984.

Sports Illustrated. Los Angeles: Time, 1954- . (Periodical).

Strunk, William, and E. B. White. *The Elements of Style.* 3d ed. New York: Macmillan, 1979.

Terhune, Albert Payson. *Lad: A Dog.* Cutchogue, NY: Buccaneer Books, 1981.

Thomas, Lewis. *The Lives of a Cell: Notes of a Biology Watcher.* New York: Bantam Books, 1975.

Thurber, James. *Thurber's Dogs.* New York: Simon & Schuster, 1965.

———. *The Thurber Album: A Collection of Pieces About People.* New York: Simon & Schuster, 1965.

Time for Kids. New York: Time, 1995- . (Periodical).

Tolkien, J. R. R. *The Hobbit.* Boston: Houghton Mifflin, 1966.

Trager, James, ed. *The People's Chronology: A Year-by-Year Record of Human Events from Prehistory to the Present.* New York: Holt, Rinehart & Winston, 1979.

Tripp, Rhoda Thomas, ed. *The International Thesaurus of Quotations.* New York: Harper & Row, 1987.

Viorst, Judith. *If I Were in Charge of the World & Other Worries.* New York: Macmillan, 1981.

Waddell, Marie L., Robert M. Esch, and Roberta R. Walker. *The Art of Styling Sentences: 20 Patterns for Success.* 3d ed. Hauppauge, NY: Barron's Educational Series, 1993.

Waldhom, Arthur, Olga S. Weber, and Arthur Zeiger, eds. *Good Reading.* 22d ed. New York: New American Library, 1986.

Wallechinsky, David, Irving Wallace, and Amy Wallace. *The Book of Lists.* New York: Little, Brown, 1995.

Weisberg, Robert. *Creativity: Genius and Other Myths.* New York: W. H. Freeman, 1986.

Whissen, Thomas. *A Way with Words—A Guide for Writers.* New York: Oxford University Press, 1982.

White, E. B. *Essays of E. B. White.* New York: Perennial Library, 1979.

Winokur, Jon, ed. *Writers on Writing.* Philadelphia: Running Press, 1986.

Wonder, Jacquelyn, and Priscilla Donovan. *Whole-Brain Thinking: Working from Both Sides of the Brain to Achieve Peak Job Performance.* New York: William Morrow, 1984.

The Writer. Boston: The Writer, 1887- . (Periodical).

Writer's Digest. Cincinnati, OH: Writer's Digest, 1921- . (Periodical).

Writer's Market, 1998: Where and How to Sell What You Write. Cincinnati, OH: Writer's Digest Books, 1997.

Wye, Margaret Enright. *The Complete Guide to Punctuation: A Quick-Reference Deskbook.* New York: Prentice Hall Press, 1986.

The Yankee. Dublin, NH: Yankee, 1884- . (Periodical).

Zavatsky, Bill, and Ron Padgett, eds. *The Whole Word Catalogue 2: A Unique Collection of Ideas and Materials to Stimulate Creativity in the Classroom.* New York: Teachers & Writers Collaborative (McGraw-Hill Paperbacks), 1977.

Zinsser, William. *On Writing Well: An Informal Guide to Writing Nonfiction.* New York: Harper & Row, 1985.

Zoobooks. San Diego, CA: Wildlife Education, 1983- . (Periodical).

Index

About the Authors

Beth Means is a freelance writer from Seattle, Washington. Known for her funny computer manuals, Beth also writes newsletters, speeches, websites, and technical papers. In her spare time, she likes writing fiction, backpacking, skiing, and quilting.

Lindy Lindner has been an Instructional Resource Teacher at Mrachek Middle School in Aurora, Colorado for 22 years. When not teaching or writing, Lindy enjoys woodcarving, hiking, and fishing with her husband and family.

from **Teacher Ideas Press**

JOURNAL KEEPING WITH YOUNG PEOPLE
Barbara Steiner and Kathleen C. Phillips

Discover a myriad of fascinating possibilities for journal keeping as a tool for transformation and for building skills. Techniques range from writing about a first memory to designing a dream house. Guidelines, tips, and lists of additional resources abound. **Grades 4–9.**
xiii, 157p. paper ISBN 0-87287-872-4

U.S. HISTORY THROUGH CHILDREN'S LITERATURE
From the Colonial Period to World War II
Wanda J. Miller

Enhance the study of U.S. history with historical fiction and nonfiction. Stepping back in time to experience a character's dilemmas, thoughts, feelings, and actions helps students easily grasp and retain a true understanding of an era. Here is all the material you need to begin a literature-based history program. **Grades 4–8.**
xiv, 229p. 8½x11 paper ISBN 1-56308-440-6

THE POET'S PEN
Writing Poetry with Middle and High School Students
Betty Bonham Lies

A wealth of ideas, advice, and examples to help bring poetry and poetry writing into the classroom! Twelve detailed lessons offer practical advice on teaching the technical aspects of poetry, suggest ways to revise work and overcome writer's block, and discuss how to integrate poetry writing with other parts of the curriculum. **Grades 6–12.**
xvi, 201p. paper ISBN 1-56308-111-3

WHAT A NOVEL IDEA!
Projects and Activities for Young Adult Literature
Katherine Wiesolek Kuta

Designed around the new language arts standards (reading, writing, representing, viewing, speaking, and listening), these stimulating activities for novels create opportunities for students to develop skills and become better readers, writers, and speakers. **Grades 7–12.**
ca.160p. 8½x11 paper ISBN 1-56308-479-1

THE INVENTIVE MIND IN SCIENCE
Creative Thinking Activities
Christine Ebert and Edward S. Ebert II

More than 50 mind-stretching activities integrate creativity and invention into the science curriculum. Help your students use their imaginations and problem-solving skills as they explore concepts articulated with word games, visual puzzles, and other reproducible projects. **Grades 4–8.**
xii, 241p. 8½x11 paper ISBN 1-56308-387-6

For a FREE catalog or to place an order, please contact:

Teacher Ideas Press
Dept. B9914 · P.O. Box 6633 · Englewood, CO 80155-6633
1-800-237-6124, ext. 1 · Fax: 303-220-8843 · E-mail: lu-books@lu.com

Check out the TIP Web site!
www.lu.com/tip